A Life with Roses

A Life with Roses

David Ruston

with Sue Zwar

ROSENBERG

First published in Australia in 2011
by Rosenberg Publishing Pty Ltd
PO Box 6125, Dural Delivery Centre NSW 2158
Phone: 61 2 9654 1502 Fax: 61 2 9654 1338
Email: rosenbergpub@smartchat.net.au
Web: www.rosenbergpub.com.au

National Library of Australia Cataloguing-in-Publication entry:

Author: Ruston, David, 1930-
Title: A life with roses / David Ruston.
Edition: 1st ed.
ISBN: 9781921719097 (hbk.)
Notes: ncludes index.
Subjects: Ruston, David, 1930-
          Rose growers--Australia--Biography.
          Rose culture--Australia.
          Floriculturalists--Australia--Biography.
          Floral decorations--Pictorial works.

Dewey Number: 635.933734092

Jacket photographs: Front: David's cast-iron container is filled with bronze *Cotinus* 'Royal Purple' to tie in with the colour of the figurine. The highlight is a mass of striped 'Camille Pisarro', one of Delbard's best roses. These are combined with apricot spuria iris and a few kniphofias. Back: An arrangement David made in New Zealand using his silver tea urn, delphiniums, iris, cornflowers, the bourbon rose 'Paul Ricault', salvia, foxgloves, watsonias and hollyhocks. *(Photograph courtesy James Manifold.)*

Backflap: David Ruston and Sheenagh Harris with the sculpture *A Life in Flowers*.

Frontispiece (pages 2 & 3): In 2002 the theme of the Renmark Rose Festival was 'Rose Arranging Through the Ages' and I volunteered to do the Flemish flower painters. On the easel is a copy of a painting by Jan Frans van Dael (1764–1840). I hung prints by other Old Masters on the walls, and brought together an amazing collection of flowers and fruits in authentic containers, using a few artificial peonies and a fritillaria or two to help me out. After all, the Old Masters painted flowers and fruits from all seasons. It took them a whole year to accomplish a masterpiece and their flowers were never in water.

All photographs are by David Ruston or John Zwar unless otherwise credited.
Set in 10 on 12 point Adobe Garamond Pro
Printed in China by Everbest Printing Co Limited

Contents

Acknowledgments

There are many people who played a part in the production of this book, the making of which was first suggested in 2007. It has grown from being a book about flower arranging to something much bigger and I hope more readable because of this.

Firstly thanks must go to Sue Zwar who has spent countless hours typing up my illegible handwriting, suggesting subject matter and editing the book. She and her husband, John, have travelled over much of the countryside so that John could photograph my flower arrangements, and many of the photos that are in the book have been taken by him. This book would not have been possible without their generous assistance.

George Davies kindly agreed to the initial formatting and also scanned my old photographs so that they could be used despite their condition. His knowledge of computers and printing techniques has been invaluable.

Patricia Routley saved me countless hours through her ready access to lists, her general knowledge and her eagle eye when it came to spelling errors.

Several people provided photographs that are included in the book. The family of the late James Young generously allowed me to use photographs from James' vast library. James Manifold and Richard Fewster came to the rescue on several occasions when specific roses or arrangements had to be photographed. Included also are photographs from Margaret Furness, Marjorie Todd and Melanie Trimper.

I would also like to mention the following people who in various ways through their generous encouragement, advice or assistance with flowers have helped in the production of this book. They include Ailsa Allen, Judy Barrett, Jacqui Davies, Walter and Kaye Duncan, Di Durston, Andrew Govanstone, Sheenagh Harris, Danny Hoffmann,

Coleen and David Houston, Jane Kaydor, Holly Kerr Forsythe, Betty McKee, Anne Ruston, Deirdre and Ken Swan, Thomas for Roses, Audrey Tonkin, Kelvin Trimper, Billy West, June Westhoff, Patricia and Roy Wilhelm and Shirley Yates.

Finally, the helpful, patient and good-humoured advice and assistance that was given by publisher, David Rosenberg, and editor, Anne Savage, both of whom expertly guided Sue Zwar and me through the tangled web of book production, was really appreciated.

Dedicated to the late Eric Trimper,
my friend for over sixty years

My cast-iron container is filled with bronze *Cotinus* 'Royal Purple' to tie in with the colour of the figurine. The highlight is a mass of striped 'Camille Pisarro', one of Delbard's best roses. These are combined with apricot spuria iris and a few kniphofias.

Foreword

This is the story of a man whose whole life has been intertwined with flowers. David Ruston was born in Renmark in South Australia's Riverland and grew up on a fruit orchard, eventually becoming one of the world's most respected rosarians. David tells his fascinating tale in a modest and unassuming way. He has coupled this with photographs and descriptions of some of the flamboyant and unusual flower arrangements that he has made in most continents of the world, over a period of many years.

Anyone who has sat in the audience while David demonstrated his proficiency with flowers would know what an accomplished entertainer he is. With seemingly effortless skill he pokes flowers in at every angle all the while regaling his spellbound audience with amusing anecdotes and knowledgeable comments about the individual flowers he is using. His imitation of 'the Old Masters' is his specialty and the information he imparts about those painters and the flowers they used is amazing, especially as his hands are also moving at top speed creating a beautiful masterpiece.

David's accomplishments are many, involving every aspect of the world of roses as well as other flowers. From his teenage years he has been a passionate exponent of roses, beginning with extending his father's rose plantings of 500 bushes to the eventual 50 000 bushes covering eleven hectares. This world acclaimed garden, the largest private collection of roses in the southern hemisphere, has been officially recognised as the National Collection of Roses in Australia. Although he has now handed its custodianship over to his niece Anne Ruston, and her husband Richard Fewster, he continues to take a vital interest in growing roses. At present he is busy developing a display garden housing old and rare roses, especially teas, Chinas and their relatives.

He has served on many committees over many years – President of the National Rose Society of Australia (1986), President of the

World Federation of Rose Societies (1991–1994), the Foundation President of Heritage Roses in Australia (1991–1993), President of the Renmark Garden Club, a position he held for a total of thirty-two years, and in 1996 the Foundation President of the Chaffey Branch of the Rose Society of South Australia. His most recent position is Chairman of the World Federation of Rose Societies Heritage Rose Committee which he has held since 2008.

In 1966 David received his first major award, the T.A. Stewart Memorial Award. T.A. Stewart was the editor of the *Australian and New Zealand Rose Annual* and the *Australian Rose Annual* from 1928 until 1946. The recipient of this award is to be 'a person who is deemed to have given outstanding service to the Rose in Australia or in New Zealand.'

The Australian Rose Annual (1967, page 40) described his achievement:

> Mr Ruston is one of the best known rosarians in Australasia. He lectures and judges frequently in various centres. He exhibits regularly at rose shows, often staging over twenty exhibits at one show. He has probably the finest, largest and most varied rose garden in Australia.
>
> Mr Ruston has made an outstanding contribution to rose growing in Australia and New Zealand and fully deserves this high honour.

The Gold Medal, an Australian Rose Award introduced in 1977 for 'outstanding Service to the Rose', was presented to David in 1982. In the same year life membership was conferred on him by the Rose Society of South Australia in recognition of his long and valued service to the cause of the rose. He has also received life memberships from the Renmark Agricultural and Horticultural Society, the Renmark Garden Club, Garden Clubs of Australia, the National Rose Society of Australia, the Royal National Rose Society, the American Rose Society, the India Rose Society and Heritage Roses of Australia.

In 1984 David was awarded an OAM in the Queen's Birthday List for 'Service to Floriculture'. This meant a great deal to him as he is an avid royalist and great admirer of Queen Elizabeth.

The World Federation of Rose Societies recognised David's contribution to the world scene of roses when it awarded him the Gold Rose Pin in 1988.

But the oldest and most prestigious award in the Rose World is that given by the Royal National Rose Society of England, the Dean Hole

Medal. This was named for the first and longest serving President of the Royal National Rose Society, the Reverend S. Reynolds Hole, Dean of Rochester, who was in office from 1877 until 1904. Some years after his death the Dean Hole Medal was instituted in his honour and David Ruston received this award in 1994.

Four Dean Hole medallists, Dr Sam McGredy from New Zealand and David Ruston, with the late Dick Balfour and Mike Roberts, both from the United Kingdom, pictured together in New Zealand in 2001.

Patricia Wilhelm, the then President of the Rose Society of South Australia, wrote in *The Australian Rose Annual* (1995, page 25):

> The Dean Hole Medal has been awarded to David Ruston in recognition of his outstanding service to the Rose over many years and for his great work as President of the World Federation of Rose Societies.
>
> The first award was made in 1909 to Rev. J.H. Pemberton, an outstanding English Rosarian. The first Dean Hole Medal to be awarded to an Australian, Alister Clark, was not until 1936. In 1952 Dr A.S. Thomas was awarded this medal. Then we have a period of forty-two years before another Australian Rosarian, David Ruston, is chosen as being a worthy recipient of this high honour.

The Deane Ross Memorial Award was initiated in 1993 by Heritage Roses in Australia to honour Deane Ross, a great South Australian rosarian, who died earlier that year. David was presented with this award in 1997 for his outstanding contribution to heritage roses.

Ian Spriggs, editor of *The Australian Rose Annual,* wrote in 2005 (page 82) after David had received yet another award, this time the

Gold Medal, from the World Federation of Rose Societies:

At the opening ceremony of the 2004 WFRS Regional Convention in Auckland, New Zealand, President, Dr Tommy Cairns bestowed on Mr David Ruston the World Federation of Rose Societies' highest award, the Gold Honor Medal.

In paying tribute to Mr. Ruston, Dr. Cairns mentioned his many achievements in the rose world including his wonderful collection of roses at Renmark and described David as 'a truly great Australian'.

It was a most moving ceremony presented so beautifully by Dr. Cairns and a fitting tribute to David who has done so much for roses over so many years.

However, a still greater honour was bestowed on David in June 2009 by the World Federation which Melanie Trimper describes in *The Rose Society of South Australia Inc. Bulletin* (Spring edition 2009, page 10):

At the fifteenth WFRS Convention, held in Vancouver in June 2009, the highest award bestowed by the Federation, the President Emeritus Award, was presented to David Ruston by World President Dr Gerald Meylan for his life-long passion, service and dedication in a variety of roles.

David Ruston's contribution to the rose has made him a world rose industry icon. His efforts have been lauded and recognised throughout Australia and internationally. David has lectured and demonstrated flower arranging at rose conferences around the world. The fact that he has been granted no less than nine life memberships to Rose Societies and Garden Clubs is a testament to his skills, creativity and generosity.

This award is held by only two living rosarians at any one time for life's duration. David now shares the honour of this award with the Baroness Lily de Gerlache de Gomery of Belgium, who was instrumental in forming the World Federation of Rose Societies in 1968. When he was presented with this accolade he received an immediate standing ovation and the event rendered him quite speechless and emotionally overcome! He never imagined he would ever receive such an honour.

David is uniquely brilliant in his field. Using his knowledge, skills and creativity he generously supports local, national and international communities and organisations, donating his time, flowers and expertise for a variety of charities. His enthusiasm to impart his specialist knowledge without obligation has been a hallmark of his life.

On 16 October 2010, in David's home town of Renmark, a sculpture depicting his life in flowers was unveiled by Sheenagh Harris, President of the World Federation of Rose Societies, who said:

David Ruston with the President Emeritus Award and Walter Duncan, two South Australians receiving awards at Vancouver.

(Photograph courtesy Melanie Trimper)

For me this is one of the greatest privileges that I could possibly experience. This is David's day and I don't believe I will ever again feel as honoured as I do here today.

The plaque accompanying the sculpture.

David giving his speech after the unveiling.

I have admired and looked up to David for many years – long before I ever met him – and I never dreamt I would one day have the opportunity to pay homage to him in this way. David is Australian and you in Australia may claim him as yours but believe me, we in the rose world believe he belongs to all of us.

There is something I would like to add to David's many accolades and that is his friendship with roses. One of my earliest recollections of this great rose lover is of him bending down to greet a rose in the most flattering terms. He greeted those beautiful blooms as if they were long lost friends and it struck me then that this true love of the Queen of Flowers showed us a man who never worked towards or looked for accolades. They came to him because of his devotion to this most favourite of flowers.

What greater accolade could be given to this great man than the David Ruston sculpture, a permanent reminder honouring his achievements and recognising the work he has done?

Sue Zwar

David Ruston and Sheenagh Harris with the sculpture *A Life in Flowers*.

Chapter 1

My Life with Flowers

In all places, then, and in all seasons,
    Flowers expand their light and soul-like wings,
Teaching us, by most persuasive reasons,
    How akin they are to human things.

from 'Flowers', in *Voices of the Night,* 1839, Henry Wadsworth Longfellow (1807–1882)

I was born in Renmark in the very early hours of 7 March 1930, a short time after my identical twin brother John, who was born just before midnight – resulting in the two of us having different birthdays.

My father, Cuthbert Sowerby Ruston, known as Rusty to all his friends, migrated from England in 1911 when he was twenty one, and came to the new River Murray irrigation settlement called Renmark. At the outbreak of the First World War in 1914 he enlisted in the 27th Battalion, fought at Gallipoli and later joined the Royal Flying Corps. After peace was proclaimed he returned to Renmark in 1919. In 1924 he married my mother, Louise Marjorie Hopkins, grand-daughter of the Reverend Ridgeway Newland who migrated to Australia in 1838 on the *Sir Charles Forbes,* the second ship that sailed to South Australia, soon after the *Buffalo,* which arrived with Governor Hindmarsh in 1836. The Reverend was a Congregational minister and the Newland Memorial Church in Victor Harbor is named after him.

My mother, aged thirty. This photo was taken shortly before her marriage to my father, to send to my father's British relatives who were anxious to see what the prospective bride from the colonies looked like. My mother had told him that she was twenty-nine and when it was revealed during the wedding ceremony that she was really thirty, my father said, in his best English voice, 'You bloody liar!'

My father during World War II in his RAAF uniform.

My parents being introduced to Prince Phillip and Queen Elizabeth in 1954.

After the fall of Singapore in World War II my father joined the Royal Australian Air Force at the age of fifty-two. He later told me that the initial intense physical training he had to undergo nearly killed him. Mother's brother and sister-in-law, both doctors, were interned in Changi which I think led to Father's decision to enrol despite his age. In his absence my job was to look after the garden which had become very overgrown with a huge impenetrable thicket of Alister Clark roses. These had to be burnt in order to make the garden more manageable. The size of the butts made me think that rosewood furniture was made from rose trunks!

For over thirty years Father was chairman of many organisations. One of these was the Renmark Irrigation Trust, which had control of the rural area around Renmark. The Renmark Council and the mayor dealt with the town. In this capacity, as chairman of the Trust, in 1954 my father, and my mother, with Mayor Stan James and his wife Ella, welcomed Her Majesty Queen Elizabeth and Prince Phillip to Renmark, a memorable occasion.

Father was responsible for establishing the local broadcasting station 5RM and he was a weekly broadcaster for many years. A brilliant speaker, he never used notes. He was also very involved with the Australian Dried Fruit Board and the Liberal and Country League. Once he told a minister in the Labor Party that, 'he had a very firm grasp of the obvious!' In 1957 Father was awarded an Order of the British Empire for services to local administration and horticulture. He died in 1970.

My mother told me that John and I talked to each other in an indecipherable language until we were eight years old. She was so concerned that she took us to a specialist where we gabbled away to each other in a corner. The specialist reassured her with the comment that 'I think they will be all right as they are not exactly dumb, are they?' We have not stopped talking since. John is very mechanically minded, probably inherited from the Ruston and Hornsby side of the family. He is also interested in vintage cars, whereas I am hopeless at anything that is technical. As a mechanic he fixes up everything that I break often with a look of despair and the question, 'What will be broken next?'

John married Joy Seekamp in 1958 and moved away from home but, fortunately for me, only a short distance, as they live on the far side of the property. I stayed on in the family home with my mother

Me and my twin John (right), aged three, with our new tricycles. We were unable to manage the pedals, preferring to put our feet on the ground to move along.

John and I (left), five years old, in our father's rose garden.

for many years. However, in 1981 she broke her leg and spent the last six years of her life in the nursing home attached to the Renmark Hospital. She died in 1987 aged ninety-three.

I became interested in plants at a very early age. My father grew three hundred rose bushes in the garden and my brother and I ate all the rose buds within reach. Roses must be in our blood as 'Ruston' is a derivation of 'Rosethorn'. I had my own garden from the age of eight and started helping with the roses soon afterwards.

When I attended Renmark High School I planted and maintained the school rose garden which lasted a number of years after I left school. I attended Adelaide High School in 1947 for my matriculation and then studied an Arts course at Adelaide University for a year. Six years of Latin and French were very handy with all those botanical names in Latin and the hundreds of roses bred in France.

Not liking city life with no plants to care for, I decided to come home to work on the fruit property and start planting roses, commencing in 1950 when I replaced some of the roses around the house that my father had planted in 1922. In winter I used to prune vines and fruit trees all day and then remove weeds from the irrigation

John and I (left) at our our seventieth birthday celebrations.

channels at night and plant new roses, all done with a lantern for light. After I'd filled up a kilometre or so of channel bank with hybrid teas and floribundas, florists began coming to me for cut flowers and the cut flower business began. I also opened up a florist's business in a rustic old shed to use surplus roses and other flowers. This led to selling budwood to rose nurseries all over Australia. Thus my hobby became my business, named Flora Rusticana in later years.

In 1956 Renmark had its biggest flood since European settlement. Both the Darling and the Murray rivers were in flood for eight months. Each day the water level would rise about an inch until it eventually peaked at 30 feet 7¾ inches (14.5 m), by which time it had inundated much of the country around the township. There were levee banks built around many properties but our bank collapsed just before the river peaked. We had managed to put a bank an extra 2 feet (60 cm) high around the house and garden a few days beforehand. Although this didn't hold, after ten days of shovelling I was able to keep the water back sufficiently so that we could then pump out all that remained. Fortunately it was winter when many plants were dormant and luckily we had few losses. Our fruit property of vines and fruit

One of the grassed walkways lined with daylilies and 'Sonia' roses on the right and 'Vienna Woods' on the left. The dog, Joe, was a trusted friend of the brilliant photographer James Young, who died tragically at the zenith of his career. He took most of the photographs for his four books on roses in the garden here, and he was one of the first professional photographers to use a digital camera for his work.

(Photograph courtesy James Young family)

trees was flooded for six weeks but survived. My parents were then in their sixties and had to be rescued by an army duck when the levee broke. For the first time my Japanese iris, which grow naturally in water, flowered well. After the floods subsided I added a long grassed rose walk to the garden which contained about a thousand bushes and this area is still flowering very well.

In 1970 after my father died I purchased the home patch of eight acres from the family and over the next six years this was filled with roses used for cutting and for budwood. Bushes were planted a metre apart in long rows with a metre and a half between each row. There were six rows in each section so that the bushes could be sprayed with a tractor towing an automatic spraying machine covering three rows at a time. A three and a half metre grassed track divided each section of six rows. A winding country road bordered the eastern side of the property and this was screened by a high fence of climbing and rambling roses. A curved irrigation channel bordered the other sections which meant that all the rows of roses were of different lengths helping to give the garden a more informal country look especially as there were lots of bulbs and perennials at the ends of each row. These were needed for flower arrangements as well as garden colour. The rose garden eventually covered twenty-seven acres.

One of the most picturesque areas in the garden was developed in 1976 on a site sheltered by old red gums and box trees next to Bookmark Creek. A pond was dug out on sloping land to house waterlilies, papyrus and bog plants and surrounded by trees and shrubs including a magnificent Mexican bald cypress, *Taxodium mucronatum*, a collection of crab apples, a weeping elm, a silver leafed pear, *Pyrus salicifolia*, and *Pyrus paisha*, now huge, about 40 feet (18 m) across. Nearby, next to an irrigation channel, I planted a red oak, *Quercus rubra*, which is now enormous and turns a magnificent golden brown in autumn. A variegated elm and some poplars also line the channel. An archway of the rambler 'Bloomfield Courage' is spectacular each October when it is awash with its clusters of red single blooms and it is then a popular backdrop for wedding photographs.

Between my old home and the new Ruston Visitor Centre an area of five acres was planted between 1982 and 1986. This included ten rows of the orange-red 'Ilona', which have been replaced with David Austin roses for cutting as orange-red was no longer popular.

There are over forty roses bearing the Bloomfield name, the name of the breeder's estate in Pennsylvania. 'Bloomfield Courage', with its single red flowers, is probably the best known and it makes a spectacular showing in spring for four to six weeks but does not repeat. This archway leading to the waterlily pond (which has been dry ever since the drought began in the late 1990s) is one of the highlights in the garden when it flowers. The cascading shoots are trimmed back after flowering. An old iron urn on a plinth in front of a clump of variegated bamboo adds to the effect, as does the variegated form of the desert ash in the background on the left.

(Photograph courtesy James Young family)

From 1994 to 1996 what is known as the Austin patch was planted as Austins became fashionable flowers for florists, particularly for use in weddings. It was fun matching the roses required to pieces of wedding fabric.

On the far side of the Visitor Centre six acres were filled with more roses for cutting and a row of trees and shrubs provided a windbreak from the north. The apple patch was planted nearby, sitting behind the roadside hedge of climbing roses planted back in 1957. The banksia roses, 'Mermaid' and 'Cl. Lorraine Lee' have to be hedged every four or five years when they spread too close to the road leading to the Visitor Centre. Included here is a collection of hybrid musk and shrub roses with a couple of medlars and old-fashioned quinces to give extra interest. A row of Granny Smith apple trees, many acting as supports for old climbing roses, acts as a backdrop to the northern end of the property.

Finally, there is the cutting shed area where apricots and peaches used to be cut preparatory to drying. This is at the end of the road

During the 1960s the rose world discovered a new group of roses called 'English roses' or what many people prefer to call 'David Austin roses', named after the man who successfully hybridised the old European roses with present day hybrid teas and floribundas, producing the form, fragrance and general characteristics of the old roses along with the remontancy of modern roses. Many of these roses have great charm and I find that they are a great alternative to the once-flowering roses when I have to demonstrate in the autumn. 'Graham Thomas' is one of David Austin's most popular roses. Here two bushes cover a wooden arch in the David Austin walk. Although it is classed as a shrub in England, in Australia it is often treated as a climber due to its great vigour. A second arch in the background is smothered with the white 'Rambling Rector', an old *Rosa multiflora* hybrid. We will never know whether it was named after a rector who went on long country walks or whether he preached too long a sermon.

(Photograph courtesy James Young family)

past my home. The shed is covered by a huge bush of *Rosa fortuneana*, smothered each year with thousands of double white flowers in early spring – the first rose to flower. It was planted in 1960 when a central area of grass was used for drying the apricots and peaches. This area then became home to a collection of old garden roses – gallicas, centifolias, damasks, albas, mosses, bourbons, hybrid perpetuals and Portlands—many of which, sadly, have died over the past ten years because of the shortage of water. The area is protected by a huge cottonwood tree, and is to be replanted during 2011 with old and species roses. A boundary fence was planted in 2010 with twenty-five rambling roses and the beginning of a collection of bourbons is soon to be added.

My favourite climbing rose, planted in 1950 and growing over a disused chemical shed near the house, is *Rosa laevigata*, a single white

Rosa laevigata.

David Ruston, aged thirty-eight, at the inaugural meeting of the World Federation of Rose Societies in London in 1968.

flower with glorious golden stamens and beautiful shiny green foliage that is evergreen. It also flowers early with the wisterias.

Watering throughout those years consisted of flood irrigation with a furrow between each row. The water supply was turned off when it reached the end of the row and this, coupled with the manure which was spread, resulted in enormous growth. Many of the cut flower varieties like 'Mr Lincoln', 'Christian Dior', 'Peter Frankenfeld', 'Pascali', 'Dr A. J. Verhage' and 'Eiffel Tower' formed large hedges by the end of the season.

I think that the garden reached maturity from about 1980. The climbing and rambling roses had grown to an enormous size, the pillar roses and arches scattered throughout the garden gave height to the flat landscape, and furrow irrigation ensured that there was ample water. There were then 50 000 bushes of 5000 varieties and at that stage the weaker growers had not deteriorated due to age. Such roses as the arch of 'Bloomfield Courage', the huge cascade of 'Adelaide d'Orleans' from an apple tree, the four rambling 'Mermaid' entanglements, the banksia roses, *Rosa laevigata*, *R. fortuneana* and the wrongly named 'Parks Yellow Tea-scented China' all opened the rose season in early September, a month before the hybrid teas began their display. Last to flower were 'Aimée Vibert' and *Rosa setigera* in early December, giving four months of colour in all. The rigid water restrictions from 2004 took a toll on the old roses and many cold-climate trees and we lost rare specimens that I had collected over many years. Saddest of all was the loss of a grove of deciduous magnolias which I had loved to use in arrangements.

In 2003 I sold my business to my niece Anne Ruston and her husband Richard Fewster. Because of water restrictions the whole garden was converted to a drip system, a huge and expensive undertaking. The spectacular Ruston Visitors Centre was built in 2005 and Rustons Roses has entered a new phase in its development.

I have retained just over an acre of garden around my home, which was built by my parents and where I have lived all my life. A few varieties of roses and other plants from my father's garden, planted in 1922, remain in front of the house. One notable survivor is 'Constance', a Pernetiana rose raised by Pernet Ducher in 1915. It was thought to be extinct until I was able to reintroduce it into commerce. It is an important rose as an ancestor of the classic rose 'Peace'. It was planted by my father in memory of his mother, Constance. Others still remaining after nearly eighty years are 'Mme Jules Grolez', bred by Guillot in 1896, 'Old Gold', bred by McGredy in 1913, and my favourite tea rose, the lovely 'Lady Hillingdon', cream in summer heat and apricot in spring and autumn. She was bred by Lowe & Shawyer, released in 1910 and named after Alice Lady Hillingdon, wife of the second Baron Hillingdon of Hillingdon Court in Uxbridge where Lowe & Shawyer had their nursery. There is also a bush of 'Mme Jules Bouché' – a very soft cream flushed pink in the centre and bred in France by Croibier in 1910. It was a popular rose for many years and, although not often seen in gardens today, it is still available in many countries.

My father also planted a lot of trees closely round the house for shade. A huge Norfolk Island pine, a number of Lombardy poplars, several melias and a lemon-scented gum still remain as well as durantas, oleanders and plumbagos. The early settlers tried out species that would withstand heat, cold and drought. Many of these trees have reached enormous proportions and are now causing some problems, although their shade is appreciated during Renmark's long, hot summers. Under the trees I have a huge collection of pots (because of root competition) where I grow hundreds of clivias and camellias, iris, daylilies, delphiniums, polyanthus, kniphofias, spring bulbs and my latest passion, salvias and succulents. Many plants such as valerian, hypoestes, poppies, sunflowers, larkspurs, forget-me-nots

A simple bowl of roses which contains a mixture of early hybrid tea roses – 'Eclipse' 1935 and 'Fantasia' 1943 (both yellows), 'Talisman' 1929 and 'Sutter's Gold' 1950 (both in apricot shades). Lightly pruned, these bushes are still very vigorous after over fifty years in the same position.

(Photograph courtesy James Young family)

and hollyhocks self-sow to give that cottage effect that fits in with the house and huge old trees. I also like to potter about in the shade house where ferns, begonias and species cyclamen are growing.

Part of a long rose walk in my garden near my 1922 cottage. On the left is pink 'Frolic', then red 'Frensham' with 'All Gold' behind. On the right-hand side are two bushes of cream 'White Spray', one of the best roses in the garden. Most of this part of the garden was planted in 1957. The photograph was taken in 2009, and the roses are still flourishing.

In 2007, at the suggestion of heritage rose lovers Margaret Furness and Pat Toolan, we received permission from Anne Ruston to create a collection of all the tea roses, Chinas and noisettes available in Australia. These roses were planted along an obsolete irrigation channel. The area stretches for 400 metres with two rows in front and a trellis of climbing teas and noisettes behind. This area and the garden around my home ensure that I have enough work to keep me busy and I still help with the maintenance of some of the old roses in Anne's collection

During the 1950s I became very keen on showing roses and so I started exhibiting them in Renmark, Adelaide and Melbourne in spring and autumn. Although this was hard work, entailing many hours of picking, packing, travelling and staging, it was enjoyable and I learned a lot from fellow exhibitors and made many friends from different areas of Australia. With differing climates in each state it was

With good friends Pat Toolan and Margaret Furness, standing in the tea rose collection a little over two years old.

obvious that some varieties liked cool conditions, others hot. Some roses were good in the spring and others in the autumn. And some roses performed well whatever the weather.

I spent all one memorable night packing my blooms into boxes, drove 150 kilometres to Mildura airport, flew to Melbourne, staged the roses, flew back in the evening, picked up my carry bag and drove home. I arrived at midnight to hear the telephone ringing with a very irate magistrate on the other end of the line telling me I had picked up his bag by mistake. It contained his gown and wig and had to be returned by 8 o'clock next morning or legal action would be taken!

At one Adelaide rose show there were displays of flower arrangements from various states of Australia. From Hobart there was an assortment of 'Baccara' roses that had turned a strange orange-rusty brown colour either because of very cold weather or because they were sitting in an old rusty pot. I remarked that they should look stunning when arranged, to which the arranger retorted, 'They *are* arranged!' It was hard to respond to this.

In Adelaide in the 1960s the *Advertiser* had donated a beautiful embossed silver tray for the best flower arrangement to be won three times, not necessarily in succession. Two of the lady members had won it twice and competition was hot. I then managed to win it three years in succession and Eric Trimper won it the next three years with magnificent bowls of 'Eiffel Tower', 'Mr Lincoln' and 'Baccara'. The *Advertiser* stopped giving the trophy after that.

My first tour overseas was to England with the New Zealand Rose Society in 1968. This was very special, as the World Federation of Rose Societies was initiated during this time in London at the instigation of the Belgium Rose Society President, Baroness Lily de Gerlache de Gomery.

In the early 1980s I was asked to lead a tour to England visiting rose gardens and rose shows. This was very successful and I was consequently asked to host several other tours to European rose gardens and World Federation of Rose Societies conferences. I have made many friends as a result of these tours.

Three tours to New Zealand gardens and two to Tasmania have also taken place over the years.

During most of my tours I have willingly done flower arranging lectures using locally grown blooms. This has been great fun, matching loaned containers to the selection of blooms given to me. I love to use flowers I cannot grow, as long as they are not glasshouse grown. These are often inclined to break and are very stiff. I much prefer that flowing effect which looks very much at home in old buildings.

On one occasion I was doing a demonstration of Flemish arrangements in California and a very large, very American lady in the front row could not be ignored. Every time I put a flower in she said, 'Oh, my Gawd!' in a very loud voice. It was most disconcerting until I found out afterwards that she was actually impressed – I had a terrible feeling before this that my efforts weren't meeting with her approval.

Over the past sixty years I have enjoyed prowling around second-hand and antique shops on the look-out for containers suitable for my flower arranging and have amassed a large collection of items such as tea urns, samovars, alabaster and silver vases as well as a rustic old butter churn, a milk urn and old farmyard implements. The following three photographs and explanations itemise some of those treasured articles.

Top row, left: During a heritage rose conference in Castlemaine, Victoria, I found this lovely pair of ewers made of spelter metal (a zinc alloy). Bowls can be fixed to their tops to hold flowers.

Top row, centre: When I was in England in 1968 I spent some time with an aunt who must have taken a liking to her colonial nephew, as she and a cousin very generously presented me with a cheque for my airfare. This enabled me to go hunting in antique shops – and at Tunbridge Wells in the Pantiles I purchased these male and female cast-iron figures. Friends who were working in England at the time carted them back to Australia for me by sea in one of their crates. I then fixed large containers on their tops, much to my mother's horror. An antique dealer told me that the figures had once been valuable, but my efforts had reduced their worth to a quarter of what it had been. As I have since used them hundreds of times for demonstrations, I think the sacrilege was worth it.

Top row, right: These spelter containers with their fascinating handles can be used with a block of foam wedged in the top, into which can be fixed skewers holding grapes and other fruits to give a medieval banquet look. I purchased them about forty years ago. They need a minimum of material to look effective.

Middle row, second left: I found this small brass and copper samovar in New Zealand. It is ideal for Flemish arrangements where few flowers are required.

Middle row, second right: A Japanese bronze incense burner (*c.* 1866) is ideal for small arrangements. I came across this while hunting through an antique shop in Melbourne. There are holes in the lid for incense to permeate. This is the kind of container that Constance Spry loved to use.

Bottom row, left: A very heavy samovar of copper is attached by four pillars to a copper and brass base. The handles of the urn emerge from monkey-like faces that are repeated in miniature at the tops of the pillars. I found it in a shop in Brighton just prior to the inaugural meeting of the World Federation of Rose Societies in London in July 1968. I used it for a demonstration with Julia Clements and a photograph appeared in the *Royal National Rose Annual* 1969 (see Chapter 4, page 72).

Bottom row, right: Another find, at an open-air antique fair near Bath, was this pair of slender spelter metal urns. A tin bowl glued to a round dowel which fits snugly inside each one holds flowers. This can be easily removed when the urn isn't required for flowers.

(Photograph courtesy James Manifold)

Top row, left: My silver tea urn has a fuel container at the bottom to keep the tea hot. I noticed this in the window of a wonderful antique shop in Penola, South Australia, when I happened to be walking past.

Top row, centre: In Lyon, France, I found a lovely alabaster urn in an antique shop I was fossicking through. I carried it through Europe in the bus while I was looking at gardens. To get it home I found a large cardboard box to pack it in, emptied my suitcase of all my clothes (which then acted as packing around the urn), put my briefcase and overnight bag in the suitcase and got home without paying for excess baggage. Three of us went shopping in Paris to buy a ball of string to secure the box. Three hours later we finally found out what we needed – *une boule de ficelle.*

Top row, right: A reproduction marble and brass set of scales with cherubims at the base holds two glass bowls hanging from a cross-piece at the top. This is ideal for short-stemmed flowers such as small spring bulbs, polyanthus and sprays of hellebore.

Bottom row, left: In my 1968 visit to England I discovered this beautiful silver épergne in Shepherd's Market in London. Unfortunately the silver centrepiece and the glass bowl it supported had been thrown out, so I added a shallow circular pewter bowl to replace the original.

Bottom row, second from left: This small alabaster bowl, given to me many years ago by an elderly friend who had prints of the Old Masters in her Victorian sitting room, sparked my interest in the history of flower arranging.

Bottom row, second from right: In London I also discovered this old silver alloy and glass J36
Victorian centrepiece. It suits a dining room table and looks lovely when teamed with old garden or Austin roses.

Bottom row, right: I found this more modern alabaster-like container recently in a Victoriana antique shop. The style is influenced by the art nouveau school of the 1920s where curves and curlicues were all the rage. It needs minimal material to look effective.

(Photograph courtesy James Manifold)

Now that I have reached the ripe old age of eighty, I realise how important the friendships I have made with people from all over the world are to me. It is fun to see the way roses are grown in the different climates of the world. In Alaska roses grow as annuals while on the plains of the Ganges the best blooms appear in midwinter. In Darwin, Australia the roses are grown on mounds with trenches in between for monsoonal rain to run off quickly. Rose growers are a very happy, friendly group willing to share their knowledge with visitors. The World Federation of Rose Societies with forty member countries has done a great job in uniting seemingly disparate groups of people who all have the common bond in their love of roses.

These huge moon-shaped mesh baskets are ideal for modern arrangements, especially large autumnal work. They were a recent investment, found in Adelaide. I spray-painted two bowls a rust colour to fit inside the baskets and hold the oasis.

(Photograph courtesy James Manifold)

Chapter 2

Flower Arranging Through the Ages

Enthusiasm for growing flowers has existed worldwide for thousands of years. The ancient Egyptians used the lotus and papyrus in religious offerings and as garlands round the necks of the pharaohs when preparing them for burial; the Persians made enclosed gardens featuring shady trees and flowering plants many years before the birth of Christ; the Greeks employed garland makers to bedeck the heads of conquering heroes and athletes; the Romans poured hot water, or lit small fires, around their rose bushes to get out-of-season blooms. The first known recording of an actual flower arrangement was found in a mosaic in Hadrian's villa at Tivoli, which is said to date from the second century AD. It includes a tulip, roses, Roman hyacinth, double anemone, red carnations and a blue morning glory. It is now in the Vatican Museum.

Most information about the history of flowers comes from manuscripts, herbals, old frescoes in churches, and paintings from the thirteenth century onwards. Cut roses were first seen in some of the medieval altarpieces of the early Renaissance in Italy. Many flowers had religious significance. The madonna lily was the symbol of the virgin birth, the three standards and the three falls of the iris were associated with the holy trinity, the carnation represented divine love, the violet, humility, and the pomegranate, with its numerous seeds, virility. The spring bulbs that appear each year and die down and come again were symbols of the resurrection. The rose also symbolised divine love and the chastity of the Virgin Mary. The short life span of the flowers was a symbol of the transience of human life.

With the rise in power of the Dutch merchants in the seventeenth century, masses of goods came in from the Orient and America, including many new varieties of plants. The wealthy merchants turned to growing all kinds of exotic plants in their gardens and, wishing to show off these novelties to their friends, commissioned artists to paint arrangements of these new and very expensive blooms. These were paintings of fictitious arrangements that included flowers of all seasons – winter aconite, snowflakes, crocus, hyacinths, narcissus, tulips, marigolds, sunflowers, opium poppies, hollyhocks, roses, nerines, hibiscus and many others. They were grouped with grapes, berry fruits, plums, figs, pomegranates, Seville oranges and lemons. Seasonal reproductions were almost impossible to execute as the paintings often took more than a year to complete, the flowers being added as they became available.

The early Flemish and Dutch painters, among them Roelandt Savery (1576–1639), Ambrosius Bosschaert (1573–1621) and Jan Brueghel the Elder (1568–1625), painted an enormous number of different flowers from all seasons. In fact, in one painting Brueghel depicted one hundred and thirty species. Quite often a painting of a mixed arrangement was repeated over and over again with the difference of only one flower. The flowers were crowded together and the colours were rich and opulent. Warm reds, oranges and yellows were softened by grey foliage such as opium poppy leaves; and areas of pale colours acted as foils to the richer tones. Blue, the blue of Delft pottery, found in morning glory, iris, hyacinths and bluebells, was always used to soften the colour schemes. Short-stemmed flowers like snowflakes and hyacinths were often used, and were placed high in the arrangement, far above the water-line. These paintings cover roughly the first quarter of the seventeenth century. Bosschaert's *Flowers in a Window*, with a landscape as a background, is one of the loveliest works of the period.

These early painters divided their flowers into three groups, the largest (nearest heaven) at the top – the madonna lily, crown imperial and opium poppy (the flower of sleep), plus the sunflower and the hollyhock. In the middle were the rose, tulip, iris, hyacinth, guelder rose, carnation and later on, the auricula. At the base were the 'lowly' flowers nearest to the earth – small narcissus, species cyclamen, cornflowers, crocus, forget-me-not, jasmine, nasturtium and morning glory. Almost all these early paintings had a dark grey or black background and usually were well lit. Pale blooms were at the centre, grading out to darker ones at the edges, merging into the background.

A late Flemish arrangement, consisting of peonies, tulips, aquilegias, iris and old roses including *Rosa foetida persiana*, 'Paul Ricault' and 'Complicata'.

One of the most renowned painters of the mid seventeenth century was Daniel Seghers (1590–1661), a Jesuit priest from Antwerp. He painted only flowers and specialised in the cartouche, a garland of flowers round a religious picture. He loved roses and, in one garland, painted in 1650, the following roses have been identified: *Rosa provincialis, R. alba semi-plena, R. foetida, R. gallica, R. gallica officinalis, R. hemisphaerica, R. gallica batavica, R. rubiginosa alba* 'Duplex', *R. rubiginosa alba* 'Simplex' and *R. damascena semi-plena*. In others of his paintings we find *Rosa alba, R. foetida bicolor, R. francofurtana* (later known as 'Empress Josephine'), *R. centifolia* and 'Tuscany'. Quite a collection for 1650! At this time arrangements were all symmetrical in design but the bouquets were more natural and less crowded, with colours more coordinated than in earlier works.

In this interpretation, an easel holds a Leonardo da Vinci painting of the Madonna and Child, surrounded by a garland done in a wreath base filled with oasis and holding honeysuckle tendrils with old alba, gallica, centifolia and damask roses on short stems. Pale colours scattered throughout give lightness to the whole and dark colours give depth. It is placed on an easel as though just painted by Daniel Seghers, when there were only fifteen or twenty varieties of roses available to paint.

The greatest painter during the second half of the seventeenth century was Jan Davidzoon de Heem (1606–1684). Brightness and transparency were of supreme importance to him, and his attention to detail was extraordinary. His masterly glass vases often had droplets of water on the outer surface, reflecting objects in the room in miniature. Damaged leaves of roses and grape vines were painted with the greatest skill to give the impression of naturalness; roses in particular were painted at all stages of development. This was now the period of asymmetrical flower arrangement, with emphasis on lateral axes, naturally curving and winding stems, such as in the opium poppy and corn stalks; often a broken tulip stem would hold

A bronze and copper samovar contains an eclectic mixture of spring flowers. Blues are bearded iris, delphiniums, cornflowers and anchusa. Yellows are achillea and iris and white comes from spuria and bearded iris. At the base are grapes, pears, oranges, a brass snail and the lid of the samovar as an accessory. The arrangement is placed on a black Japanese stand on a round oak table. In these later Flemish–Dutch arrangements much use is made of fruit and accessories.

This swag arranged on an old easel is influenced by Jan Davidzoon de Heem. It consists of a flowing design of sunflower seed pods, persimmons, brown pears, rose hips, medlars, variegated lemons, crab apples and red grapes with foliage attached. The only flowers are gaillardias, which tie in well with the easel. The design is arranged in a large oval block of oasis, hung so that it cascades downwards.

Practically all the old Flemish arrangements were placed in front of dark panelling with light usually coming in from the left. Here the samovar contains foxgloves, crinum, pokers, sunflowers for that touch of yellow, blue iris, cornflowers, hollyhocks, silene, *Rosa centifolia*, scabious, a red gaillardia – the red of Rembrandt – and fruit at the base. Note how the cut oranges and kiwi fruit add to the effectiveness of the arrangement, although kiwi fruit is not authentic to the period. The use of the black stand puts the fruit on two levels to give more depth to the whole.

(Photograph courtesy James Manifold)

a prominent position in the painting. His style was copied by such painters as Abraham Mignon, but was never surpassed.

In the eighteenth century the asymmetrical flower arrangement reached its peak. Jan Van Huysum (1682–1749), Rachel Ruysch (1664–1750), Jan Van Os (1744–1808) and Gerard Van Spaendonck (1746–1822) specialised in great flowing designs placed on marble ledges, with lots of contrasts between pale and dark coloured flowers, using curved stems and creating an immense feeling of depth. Van Huysum used the large terracotta vase, enlivened by friezes of putti, for the first time. He loved bold colours – orange, reds and yellows – softened by pale peonies in the centre, and *Rosa centifolia* cascading downwards in a most natural way, opium poppies with their swirling grey foliage and striking form, with a feature of auriculas of many colours with contrasting eyes adding to the effect. Van Huysum and his many followers used fruit at the base of the container, including grapes, berry fruits – so translucent that the pips could be seen through the skin – peaches, pomegranates, figs and later on the new horticultural wonder, the pineapple! Jan Van Os painted wonderful fruit and flower pieces, with birds and reptiles as accessories, with the birds eyeing off the luscious grapes and a pineapple placed precariously high in the arrangement to show it off. Another eye-catching, slightly later study was by Georgius Van Os (1782–1861), a son of Jan Van Os, who specialised in great birds with wings outstretched, hovering at the top of a painting of flowers and fruit as though ready to gobble up the goodies below.

There has been a lot of controversy about the yellow centifolia rose now known as *Rosa huysumiana*, painted first by Van Huysum and later by Jan Van Os and then Georgius Van Os. In a letter to a friend, Van Huysum says that he had to wait for a whole year to paint the yellow centifolia, as no blooms were available. It must have been extremely rare, and a poor grower, as it disappeared fifty years after its introduction. Perhaps it was a chance cross with *Rosa foetida persiana* or *R. hemisphaerica*. We will never know, but I would like to give Van Huysum the credit for such an important discovery. It is interesting that quite a few flowers painted in this period have disappeared without trace. Some were painted in one century and then nothing

A samovar holds a collection of flowers and fruits in the style of the Old Masters. An artificial fritillaria, white peony and pink tulip are combined with fresh delphiniums, liliums, sunflowers, goldenrod and old roses, grapes, quinces and citrus. Delphiniums are a lovely spiked flower, today found in some beautiful muted pinks and mauves, cream and white, as well as every shade of blue.

was heard of them for a century or so when they reappeared once again. The arum lily, crinum, strelitzia and clivia are examples of this.

An important contribution to the history of the rose and other flowering plants was the publication of Robert Furber's catalogue in London in 1730. These prints, one for each month of the year, were painted by the Flemish artist Pieter Casteels (1684–1749), and engraved by Henry Fletcher (active 1715–44). The illustrations for the twelve months contained four hundred varieties of plants and fourteen varieties of roses, rather different from those used by Daniel Seghers one hundred years earlier. For the month of May there was the early-flowering cinnamon rose, *Rosa cinnamomea*, and the red and yellow Austrian roses. For June there was 'Maiden's Blush', 'Blush Belgique', *R. francofurtana*, *R. alba*, the moss Provence rose, the Dutch hundred-leaf rose (*R. centifolia*) and a lovely bloom of 'Rosa Mundi'. Strangely enough, the month of July contained no roses. For August there was the striped monthly rose, the influence of the Chinas being apparent for the first time. In September we have the white monthly rose, again showing the China influence. (These last two roses are

A silver tea urn containing soft-coloured flowers in the Rococo style of Louis XV and XVI, where deep pinks, beloved of Mme du Barry and Mme de Pompadour, were the rage. Here iris, delphiniums, cascading tulips, foxgloves, larkspurs, old roses and blue cornflowers tie in nicely with the gorgeous cream peonies which give impact at the centre. I find arrangements like these with lots of flowers must be replenished with water each day. I usually have a hole at the back for filling with a watering can with a long spout.

A replica of a Medici silver urn holds an assortment of the soft-toned flowers loved by such influential women as Mme de Pompadour and Mme du Barry at the French court at Versailles – iris, delphiniums and cornflowers for that touch of blue. Watsonias, valerian, cherry blossom and alba roses provide the pink shades, while white is provided by guelder roses, iris and crinum, forming a harmonious whole.

no longer available.) October gives us the late-flowering double white musk. For December there is just one little bud of the monthly rose. This important publication gives us a great deal of information about primulas, auriculas, hyacinths, anemones, carnations and campanulas, and about twenty-five plants which had recently arrived from America.

The garden at Malmaison, created by Empress Josephine, was to have an enormous influence on succeeding generations. Pierre-Joseph Redouté painted the entire collection of one hundred and eighty varieties and became known as the greatest painter of roses of all time. From his work we know for certain what was available in the first decade and a half of the nineteenth century. He depicted the first China roses, which led to the repeat-flowering roses of today and the first noisettes. The Redouté roses have been reproduced by the tens of thousands as prints, as table mats, on china and porcelain ever since and must be the most popular paintings of roses in the world today.

Until the beginning of the nineteenth century, paintings of roses featured the once-flowering varieties, nearly all in shades of white, pink, crimson and purple, with stripes of these colours. The only yellow roses were the species from Asia. With the advent of the yellow teas and noisettes in the early to mid nineteenth century the colour range expanded to include new, more subtle shades, and painters were quick to take advantage. Henri Fantin Latour (1836–1901) was the foremost painter of this era. We can recognise 'Gloire de Dijon', 'Etoile de Lyon', 'Maréchal Niel', 'Celine Forestier' and 'Cloth of Gold' in his work. He used roses alone or mixed with opium poppies, peonies, hollyhocks, larkspurs and the newly imported dahlias, asters and chrysanthemums.

Claude Monet (1840–1926) surprisingly did *not* paint roses in spite of growing them in his garden at Giverny. He favoured his beloved waterlilies, dahlias, gladioli, lilies and chrysanthemums.

The second quarter of the nineteenth century saw the end of the great voluptuous flower paintings of the Flemish, Dutch and French schools, but they have left us a marvellous legacy when it comes to massed arrangement. The bold use of colour, the sweeping S and C curves, the diagonal and lateral movement, the feeling of depth, the turning of flowers to the side and the back to give added interest,

Placed in a lovely bronze-coloured spelter figurine is a large arrangement of artificial flowers in the style of the Old Masters. Included are an artificial fritillaria (*Fritillaria fakensis*), lilies, delphinium, blue and purple iris, tulips, hollyhocks, dried achillea to give a touch of yellow, and lovely pink and white peonies. I have nicknamed these *Paeonia 'artificiala alba'* and *P. 'artificiala rosea'*. The arrangement is standing on a tall torchère and still looks good after five years, with an occasional light once-over with a feather duster. Such works can give colour to a room in winter or in the heat of summer when fresh flowers do not keep well.

A brass samovar filled with a baroque medley of orange liliums, sunflowers in yellow-brown and striped tulips, which tone in well with pomegranates and citrus at the base. The red dangling amaranthus ties in with the purple grapes and tulips. Touches of blue come from salvias and a hyacinth. 'Claire Rose' substitutes for '*Rosa centifolia*' which is only available in spring. White softens the rich colour scheme with the use of *Lilium longiflorum*, asters and a spray of 'Fair Bianca' roses. The stem of pomegranate foliage breaks the horizontal line of the top of the pedestal.

(*Right*) An old copper container holds autumn flowers which contrast well against a black background that gives a feeling of depth. Sprays of 'Graham Thomas' and 'Lamarque' roses flow out each side and are joined with long sprays of *Rosa woodsii fendleri*, a quince and a pomegranate. Blue iris, *Lilium longiflorum* and orange lilies form a silhouette at the top. Fillers are common garden perennial asters, goldenrod and blue statice. A head of 'Cardinal Hume' echoes the colours of the mauve tulips and purple grapes at the base.

the turning of leaves to show the undersides with their interesting veining and, above all, the use of great bases and plinths to show off an amazing number of accessories, whether fruit, flowers, birds' nests, stuffed birds, cut-open melons or pomegranates, can teach us all an enormous amount.

Nowadays we can find much more material when we try to arrange flowers in the style of a particular period. I find September, October and November are the best months for attempting a period arrangement. Roses, guelder roses, cherry, apple and plum blossom, narcissus, tulips, hyacinths, peonies, opium poppies, anemones, iris and jasmine can all be obtained at this time. Here in South Australia, if we have a friend in a cool Hills garden and another in a warm early spot, it all helps to amass a wide range of material. The great thing is that we only need a few bits of everything to produce a truly rich, striking and opulent display very different from the normal everyday arrangement. They are fun to do and they teach us so much about the history of plants.

Roses used during Queen Victoria's reign were mainly hybrid perpetuals, along with tea roses grown under glass. Such varieties as

A Flemish-style design in spring containing the rich red, orange and yellow colours of the baroque period softened by pale pink 'Fantin Latour' roses, sprays of guelder roses, and iris, cornflowers and salvias for that touch of blue. The dark door makes a perfect background to show off the flowers. The orange is provided by poppies and kniphofias, the yellow by sunflowers and ranunculus, and the red by double opium poppies, a species pelargonium, ornamental corn and dried pomegranates. The green comes from guelder rose, rose and poppy foliage and white from watsonias and 'Mme Hardy' and 'Frau Karl Druschki' roses. The samovar lid makes a good accessory and breaks the horizontal line of the old stand. The dark grapes and lotus pod repeat the colour of the stand.

'The Bride', 'Bridesmaid', 'Catherine Mermet' and 'Maréchal Niel' were favourites for weddings and public functions. The Victorians loved heavy colours – crimson, purples, strong yellows, acid green and magenta mixed with orange. Arrangements were packed and containers were often florid and too dominant, furniture was heavy mahogany and rooms were overfilled. The great gardener Gertrude Jekyll quipped that 'walking through a Victorian sitting room was like trying to negotiate a thicket'. Strangely enough, these bold contrasting colours are now in vogue in grouped modern work.

A Victorian cranberry glass épergne with three flutes is filled with maidenhair and sword fern. The tea roses used were all Victorian varieties: 'Mrs B.R. Cant', 'Anna Olivier', 'Monsieur Tillier', 'Homere', 'Niphetos', 'Etoile de Lyon', 'Dr Grill' and 'Catherine Mermet'.

(Photograph courtesy James Young family)

The surtout, a combination of two low containers with a central column, was popular in Edwardian times. Rambling roses were in vogue and quite often arrangements consisted of just the one variety cascading down from the centrepiece. Here deep pink 'Dorothy Perkins' is used with her pale pink sport, 'Dorothy Dennison', and 'White Dorothy Perkins', also a sport.

One thing we can thank our Victorian ancestors for is the épergne, either in silver, clear, ruby or cranberry glass or porcelain. This type of container is ideal for short-stemmed flowers on the dining room table or, if too large, on a sideboard. The 'Ellen Terry stand' was also invented by the Victorians – this allowed for low arrangements at the base and had a container on a tall stem towering above, leaving a gap between the two levels for conversing across the table. With the advent of rambling roses – 'Dorothy Perkins', 'Dorothy Denison' and 'Lady Gay' – lovely loose cascading effects from the top container could be created.

In the 1920s floral arrangements were influenced by the art nouveau movement. The flowers favoured were of the simpler kinds, reflecting an oriental aesthetic touch, and containers were curvaceous and more restrained.

In the 1940s and 1950s, Constance Spry's influence on flower arranging was enormous. Mrs Spry used great sprays of garden trees and shrubs such as lilac, flowering prunus, cherries and apples, philadelphus, autumn foliage, hops, and branches of lime blossom with the leaves stripped. Her sense of colour harmony was superb. She loved the old purple, cerise and striped gallicas and bourbons and was influential in bringing them back to gardens. She also brought back the rich colours of the Dutch and Flemish Old Masters with a rekindling of interest in old-fashioned flowers – auriculas, hollyhocks, sweet william and pinks. I consider Constance Spry (1886–1960) the pioneer of modern flower arranging. The books she wrote explaining her art are still available.

It was after World War II that English woman Julia Clements (1906–2010) started the trend for ordinary people to arrange their own flowers. This had previously been left to the head gardener. Through her influence flower arranging societies were formed and flower shows became popular. Julia Clements (later Lady Julia Clements OBE) arranged roses in various stages of development from tight bud to full bloom – a trend still popular today. She loved simple arrangements of one kind of flower. Her importance to the rose world is evident in that three roses have been dedicated to her – 'Julia Clements', a red floribunda released in 1957, 'Lady Seton', a pink hybrid tea released in 1966, and the very popular and uniquely coloured 'Julia's Rose', released in 1976. She was still giving talks at over 100 years of age. Her books are still available.

This is a fun creation. I brought several ostrich feathers to Christchurch where I did a demonstration in 1990. These had been used on a hat when a friend's mother attended a garden party in 1903 at Buckingham Palace. When I arrived at Auckland airport I went through customs worried that the ostrich feathers might be confiscated but they caused no problem. However, I had tied them to thin bamboo supports – and bamboo was a prohibited import. They were confiscated and the ostrich feathers were brought in as 'millinery'! The weather in Christchurch had been very wet and the feathers went limp. White antirrhinums, stocks, cream noisette roses and green nicotiana were used with a few white 'Lamarque' roses. But the feathers were certainly the prominent feature, a genuine Edwardian arrangement!

The 1950s were the era of the bowl and vase and trough – everyone seemed to have a silver rose bowl. Bowls and vases arranged in the round were very suitable for roses. The trough was fan-shaped in design and needed a combination of spiky flowers and round flowers with lots of airy filling. The trough was the forerunner of the pedestal arrangement of today.

The late 1960s, 1970s and 1980s were the decades of the 'modern arrangement' in which, in the right hands, a minimum of material could have a maximum effect. Bright-coloured roses such as 'Super Star', 'Montezuma', 'Fragrant Cloud' and 'Baccara' were favourites, as well as gerberas, antirrhinums, arum lilies and strelitzia. More and more dried and contorted material was being used with fewer and fewer flowers to create abstract and structural effects. Fruit, vegetables, fungi, marine material and material that could be woven was all the rage. Roses were used cut short and grouped together to provide impact of colour and form.

At a rose festival at Timaru in the South Island of New Zealand, a lovely glass container on a stand was loaned to me for my demonstration on the art nouveau period, 1920–1930. I found long, curvaceous stems of 'Constance Spry' and mixed them with the Portland rose 'Comte de Chambord', with some of the roses facing the back being reflecting in the mirror.

Constance Spry loved the subtle colour combinations of soft mauves, parchment colours and striped flowers. Here is a small tazza of the Aril-bred iris that she loved for their combination of greys, blacks, mauves and browns. These rare iris were given to me by Pat Toolan, President of the Aril Society International. They are very difficult to grow as they need extremely dry conditions over the summer months and excellent drainage.

Here a small silver formal rose bowl of a type much favoured from the 1950s contains my favourite Austin rose, 'Sophy's Rose'. Her deep pink-mauve changes to an almost violet colour and the flowers hold very well. A block of oasis extends above the rim to obtain the all-important downward flow. This arrangement was made to be viewed from all angles.

(Photograph courtesy James Manifold)

Another container of roses, this time a silver wine cooler of 'Christian Dior' with their own foliage filling out the arrangement. There is a good transition from buds to full blooms.

(Photograph courtesy James Manifold)

A tall tin container with driftwood, grey succulents and 'Chartreuse de Parme' and 'Plum Crazy' roses grouped together in a modern arrangement.

What of the future? I hope that the influence of great arrangers like George Smith, Derek Bridges and Kenneth Turner, all from the United Kingdom, and J. Gregory Conway from the United States, with their lavish use of flowers, will prevail against the former modernists. A good sign is the resurgence in the use of the bold, bright colours of the Old Masters.

Chapter 3

Special Events

One of the great pleasures in my life with roses – indeed, with all flowers – has been demonstrating flower arranging in Australia and many other parts of the world – in stately homes, for church festivals, Rose Society conferences and other exciting venues. This has led to my meeting many interesting people in many walks of life. This chapter concentrates on some highlights – from Adelaide's Ayers House in the 1970s, to the excitement of royal visits in 1986 and 2002, to the unveiling of a celebratory sculpture in Renmark in 2010.

I prefer, if possible, to use home-grown flowers, fruit and vegetables and branches of flowering trees, which give a more natural flowing look to a work. I find stiff and erect or sappy-stemmed glass-house exotics more difficult to use. Often prizes are awarded to those who have purchased the most expensive material, but I feel that those who use ordinary material in an unusual way should be commended.

It is very important to make your arrangements compatible with their surroundings. Huge rooms need big bold arrangements or they are lost, and at functions it is important that the arrangements are taller than the standing guests. Simple arrangements of cottage-type flowers can look very effective in old cottages and farmhouses, especially when you choose flowers of the same period as the dwelling. In very modern buildings and art galleries and hotels impressive results can be achieved using dramatic material such as Gymea lilies, sculptured wood, loops of wisteria vine and even old, gnarled grape vines and limbs of ivy, along with Australian xanthorrhoeas with their beautifully twisted and contorted seed heads, and huge palm spathes with wonderful textures. Such bold material can look stunning placed in huge containers like wine barrels or old-fashioned coppers, even petrol drums painted with a combination of rust and brown that does not detract from the sculptured look of the arrangement.

St Peter's Cathedral, Adelaide 1980s–1990s

On three occasions over a period of seven or eight years in the 1980s–1990s, I decorated St Peter's Cathedral in Adelaide for special events convened by Margaret Richardson, wife of the Dean. When Dean Richardson and his wife moved to Melbourne in 1999 after his appointment as Dean of St Paul's Cathedral, the lavish decorations for the different festivals celebrated during the church year were discontinued.

Harvest thanksgiving at St Peters. Three pedestals at different levels hold a mass of garden flowers. Spikes of yucca give height with sunflowers, kniphofias, gold roses, goldenrod and cumquats from my garden flowing downwards to a rustic cart filled with fruit, vegetables and grasses.

A tall tubular support on legs holds four metal bowls, all painted cream, to hold the flowers in oasis. Masses of apricot roses ('Thais', 'Copper Gem', 'Pierre B', 'Vienna Charm' and 'Just Joey') are combined with orange watsonias, Dutch and spuria iris and cream *Melaleuca linariifolia*, all brought 240 kilometres from the garden at Renmark. Matching arrangements reaching up 4 metres were placed each side of the high altar.

Ayers House, Adelaide 1970s–2009

Ayers House is the Victorian mansion of the Ayers family who were early pioneers in Australia and one of South Australia's oldest and most respected families. The home is now the headquarters of the National Trust in South Australia. My first demonstration there was early in the 1970s.

In 1982 when I was ask to demonstrate at Ayers House as part of a festival of flowers, I traced the life of an imagined Miss Ayers from her birth, to her marriage to an Englishman and finally her death, when she wanted lavish flower arrangements for a wake after her burial. With such wonderful containers available it was all very easy.

In autumn 2009 I spent several hours arranging flowers in strategic places throughout Ayers House then demonstrating before an audience as a fundraiser for the National Trust.

A Flemish arrangement of mixed flowers in a samovar with hollyhocks, iris, lilies, achillea and two magnificent apricot tree peonies given to me by Trevor Nottle from Mt Lofty. It was placed on an antique table with a beautiful old cedar door as a background. Almost all the paintings of the old masters were displayed against dark wooden panels so it was appropriate that my Flemish arrangement had such a background.

The impressive old table seating at least twenty-five people in the state dining room with the centrepiece a magnificent épergne of Broken Hill silver holding old gallica and alba roses. The two matching candlesticks are similarly adorned. This photograph, taken forty years ago, has faded but is still very important to me as part of my life arranging flowers.

Two lovely old lustre vases from Ayers House filled with old roses, accentuating the portrait above them. The flowers are a mixture of old gallicas, centifolias, albas and hybrid musks.

Ayers House dining room in 1982 with the table set for a luncheon and decorated with a ruby glass épergne filled with old roses. The mantelpiece lustre vases contain more old roses.

Arranging 'Mrs Herbert Stevens' roses in a ruby glass épergne, this time working on the veranda of Ayers House.

Another arrangement on a sideboard, done in a silver surtout often used on Victorian dining tables. Here a combination of a central column and side-pieces is filled with 'Sophy's Rose', bred by David Austin and one of my favourites. A few sprays of olive with their fruits cascade downwards. The colour of 'Sophy's Rose' deepens as the flowers age, and the blooms last very well when picked. Table arrangements often used only one variety of flower in the late Victorian and Edwardian eras.

Ayers House has several magnificent épergnes made of Broken Hill silver. This one, placed on a sideboard, contains a large centrepiece and three side-arms holding the tea rose 'Perle des Jardins', a rose bred in 1874. 'Perle des Jardins' is at its best in warm conditions; in cold climates it can ball and suffer from mildew. The arrangement is authentic to the period of the house.

An alabaster column on a sideboard in Ayers House adorned with grey olive branches and mauve 'Lady X' roses with deep pink 'Peter Frankenfeld' and purple 'Chartreuse de Parme', a strongly perfumed, many-petalled rose from Delbard.

The finished épergne in place in the dining room.

This huge arrangement contains the grey foliage of *Eucalyptus cineria*, or Argyle apple, which complements the roses 'Memoriam', 'Royal Highness', 'Shell Queen' and 'Peter Frankenfeld'. It is placed in front of a gorgeous old embossed mirror in the hall.

Royal Visit 1986

Carrick Hill is a lovely old Tudor mansion overlooking the city of Adelaide in the suburb of Springfield, where I was a member of the Garden Advisory Committee. When I heard that the Queen was to visit Carrick Hill as part of her visit in 1986 to celebrate the sesquicentennial of South Australia I offered to do the flowers, although it was early March, a bit early for good autumn roses. There was a gale blowing on the day, and the Queen could not land at Glenelg where the first ship, the *Buffalo*, arrived in 1836. This meant that the royal party had to disembark at Outer Harbour which delayed their arrival at Carrick House by nearly two hours.

I arranged flowers in all the reception rooms, mainly in autumn tones to match the ancient oak panelling brought out from England in 1939 along with the glorious staircase in the huge entrance hall. Mixed flowers toned in with a large painting of voluptuous naked maidens with a tumble of pumpkins at their feet. The Queen remarked how well I had matched the roses to the pumpkins! I remember the rose was 'Fred Howard', still a favourite of mine.

A silver punch bowl of 'Christian Dior' roses echoing the colour of the Rockingham porcelain in the Chinese cabinet. Note the painting of roses by French artist Henri Fantin-Latour (1836–1904) above the bowl.

A huge bowl of full blooms of the richly scented 'Mr Lincoln' roses – the Queen remarked on the perfume pervading the whole room.

Her Majesty also commented on the soft pink roses arranged in an old Elizabethan cot. The cot looked very hard and too uncomfortable to house a baby

Royal Visit 2002

In 2002 Queen Elizabeth officially opened the house and garden of the newly built grand complex, Chateau Barrosa at Lyndoch in the Barossa Valley – note the difference in spelling – owned by Mr and Mrs Hermann Thumm. Chateau Barrosa, situated in the heart of the picturesque Barossa, which is renowned for its quality wines, sits in a 12 hectare garden containing tens of thousands of rose bushes.

Her Majesty wore a soft yellow suit which suited her admirably. My friend, Eric Trimper, told her that she looked lovely in yellow. We were dumbfounded, but I think by her smile that she enjoyed the compliment. (Eric Trimper, Dean Stringer and I selected the roses for the enormous rose garden at Chateau Barrosa.)

It was late February, not a good time for roses, but the great day was cool. I arranged huge stone urns of just roses and grapes, which looked exactly right for the occasion, each side of the entrance. We had to fight off the birds attracted by the grapes before the royal arrival.

After the opening, when Her Majesty planted a 'Queen Elizabeth' rose, guests attended a luncheon where a member of the royal party sat at each table. We were lucky to have a lady-in-waiting at our table. Queen Elizabeth talked to us in the garden afterwards and we were all amazed at her general knowledge and sense of humour. My father was English and I have always been a royalist, even more so after meeting

Chatting with Queen Elizabeth at Chateau Barrosa.

Roses, hips, berries, grapes and grape leaves in a stone urn at the entrance to Chateau Barrosa.

Urns filled with roses, green grapes and quinces in the entrance hall at Chateau Barrosa.

one of the most remarkable women in the world today. Prince Phillip spent the day with the fishing fleet at Port Lincoln. I am sure that was a memorable day too for those present.

Rose Show, Bermuda 1994

Bermuda is an amazing island off the coast of the US state of Georgia. The climate is warm and humid in the summer and an occasional hurricane can cause damage to foliage from salt spray if there is no rain to wash it off. Many old China roses and some teas were brought in by the early settlers several centuries ago, and they are still flourishing. Most have been given local names as their original names have long been lost. The old roses grow well with no winter frosts whereas many of the modern roses decline after a few years. A tax haven for many years, Bermuda is still very British in many ways. Being a small island with a dry summer, all winter rain is collected and stored in underground water tanks to be used when water is in short supply. Bermuda's soil is very sandy but grows a lot of subtropical plants very well indeed. Some of the homes are so large that they can be mistaken for hotels. I flew to Bermuda in April 1994 to talk and demonstrate at their rose show.

Here I have arranged spring flowers with *Lilium longiflorum*, the most dominant flower, placed at the apex. It is grown commercially in Bermuda and bunches are always sent to Queen Elizabeth at Easter. Dutch iris, narcissus, a few old tea roses, anemones, a lovely green aloe, salvias and berries have also been included. The dark background shows off the flowers to perfection.

Royal Visit, Renmark 1986

Renmark, my home town on the River Murray 240 kilometres north-east of Adelaide, was lucky enough to be visited by Prince Charles and Princess Diana in 1986. It was autumn and our local garden club was asked to decorate the venue, the Renmark Community Hotel, with large urns of roses, grapes and local fruit and vegetables. In his address, Prince Charles quipped that he had never been present at a function above a drive-in liquor shop before.

One of the arrangements I made for the visit of Prince Charles and Princess Diana was a large urn of 'Thais' roses (also called 'Lady Elgin') mixed with pyracantha berries and clusters of persimmons. 'Thais' is best grown in a hot, dry climate because it is prone to black spot.

On the left, the rose 'Interview' is teamed with green tassels of *Amaranthus viridis* with a matching arrangement, partially obscured, on the right. In the centre 'Baccara' is featured in a lovely old figurine container. Note the palm spathe holding grapes and pomegranates, persimmons and quinces. The centrepiece was a huge cornucopia of local produce all pegged to a wire netting base, in case the fruit decided to roll downwards among the guests! I remember a similar arrangement in a huge cathedral in England in the comedy TV show, *The Two Ronnies* – in the middle of the service the fruit suddenly took off, a river of apples that finally rolled down the aisle into the porch.

It was with a feeling of great sadness that I decorated our Anglican church in Renmark in memory of Princess Diana after her death on 31 August 1997. Never has a death touched so many hearts all over the world.

Renmark Rose Shows 1958–1994 and Rose Festivals 1995–2010

From 1958 until 1994 Renmark was famous for its twice-yearly rose shows, held in spring and autumn. Exhibitors came from all around Victoria and South Australia for these events, which were very popular. In 1966, for example, we had 790 entries altogether; in the Rose Championship class, which asked for six distinct exhibition varieties, we received 23 entries. The Renmark Garden Club, which began in 1958, organised the shows. I have been President for thirty-two years, although not consecutively, and of course, I was very eager to promote such events.

From 1995, instead of the former twice-yearly rose shows, Renmark has hosted an annual Rose Festival in mid October. This event, which runs for about a week, has taken place every year since, despite the difficult drought conditions that the area has had to contend with.

A flowing design of 'Interview' roses in my bronze male figurine, created for the 2002 Rose Festival. This rose has long stems with only one bloom per stem and holds for over a week when picked. It is magnificent as a mature bloom but is no longer popular. This is a great pity. Note the wooden base fastened to the figurine to give added balance.

(*Left*) A part of a display for the 1999 Rose Festival, set up in the Renmark Institute. It features colour blended roses arranged in terracotta containers on pedestals of varied heights.

In 2002 the theme of the Rose Festival was 'Rose Arranging Through the Ages' and I volunteered to do the Flemish flower painters. On the easel is a copy of a painting by Jan Frans van Dael (1764–1840). I hung prints by other Old Masters on the walls, and brought together an amazing collection of flowers and fruits in authentic containers, using a few artificial peonies and a fritillaria or two to help me out. After all, the Old Masters painted flowers and fruits from all seasons. It took them a whole year to accomplish a masterpiece and their flowers were never in water.

My lovely French ewer stands on a low table and holds the Austin rose 'Jude the Obscure', which cascades downwards. Many of David Austin's shrub roses have stems that flow down gracefully, so different from the rigid stems of glasshouse ones.

(*Right*) In 2008 it was my job to do an archway of local flowers just inside the entrance to the Renmark Institute, where the arrangements were displayed. I used a metal frame painted green which contained nine ice-cream cartons filled with oasis and masses of roses, iris, nandina and trusses of green euphorbia with a background of ivy. It took four buckets of ivy to hide the

(*Below right*) To hold the floral carpet required at the foot of an iron bedstead I located a large, rectangular, very low-sided tin tank that had been used for keeping pots of Louisiana iris in water. It took twenty bricks of cut oasis to fill the tank, but with the stems placed deep into the oasis the finished product looked even better after four days. Masses of 'Angel Face', 'Madame President', 'Swan' and 'Royal Highness' were used with mauve scabious, ageratum and Queen Anne's lace. This was the work of the local flower arranging group for the 2008 Rose Festival. My contribution was the tank and a lot of the flowers.

At the 2009 Rose Festival we celebrated major events of the calendar, including the annual South Australian Bay to Birdwood car rally. My contributions were to publicise the festival with an arrangement celebrating this rally, and to create arrangements to celebrate Queen Elizabeth's birthday and the Royal Family.

For one of my tributes to Her Majesty's birthday I used a huge old urn with delphiniums, Dutch iris and long-stemmed 'Queen Elizabeth' roses with a background of dark-coloured prunus foliage.

(*Left*) To publicise the festival I decorated an old red and silver Bentley sports car with red 'Christian Dior' roses combined with silver succulents and sprays of artemisia.

(*Photograph courtesy James Manifold*)

A cast-iron figurine holds an array of 'Royal Highness' roses complimented by the silver foliage of *Adenanthos sericea*.

A general view of the display. We included arrangements of 'Princess Margaret' and 'La Reine' (in honour of Queen Victoria), 'Elizabeth of Glamis' (named after the Queen Mother's home in Scotland), 'Silver Jubilee' (named for the Queen's silver wedding), 'Golden Celebration' for her golden wedding, 'Royal William', 'Diana, Princess of Wales' and 'Duke of Windsor'.

Olivewood 2002

Olivewood, now a National Trust museum on the outskirts of Renmark, was the original home of Charles Chaffey, who in 1888 took over the management of the Renmark Irrigation Colony from his two older brothers. The spacious old home was built in 1889 of native pine slabs with deep, shady verandas. The house is usually open to the public during Renmark Rose Festivals, and in October 2002 I was asked to create several arrangements in keeping with its character.

A brass and copper samovar on an antique sideboard holds a collection of garden flowers – cherry and apple blossom, guelder roses, blue Dutch iris, old-fashioned bearded iris in lavender and blue, opium poppies and tritonias with curved stems. Yellow is provided by spuria iris. The roses are the first blooms of the season and include the centifolia 'Gros Choux d'Hollande' and the bourbon 'Mme Isaac Pereire'. At the base is a collection of fruits – a gourd, dried pomegranates, an artichoke and grapes.

(Photograph courtesy James Young family

Camawald 2004

In April 2004, during a special weekend for the South Australian Rose Society, I was asked to do a demonstration using rustic farm containers in the woolshed at John and Sue Zwar's property, Camawald, at Coonawarra in the south-east of South Australia. The venue was truly Australian, for on entering one was immediately aware of the combined aroma of sheep manure and lanoline from the fleeces that pervades all shearing sheds. Black drapery was used to hide the shearing machinery behind me. John and Sue have an extensive garden sheltered by enormous old red gums, and have amassed a large collection of old utensils, perfect for flower arrangements.

The old milk can weathered to a soft terracotta colour with the lid as an accessory was perfect for the arrangement of pokers, leucadendron, winter gladioli, 'Thais' roses and alstroemeria. The table grapes cascading downwards tie in with the burgundy leucadendron.

An old washing machine filled with very long-stemmed banksias perfectly matching the patina of the container. These are mixed with a few *Kniphofia* 'Winter Cheer'.

Weddings

Over the years I have done the flowers for a large number of weddings in churches, homes, marquees in gardens and even on the banks of the River Murray. In our climate marquees can be very hot indeed and arrangements need to be left until the last minute before being placed in position.

A wooden butter churn filled with quinces, pyracantha berries, crab-apples, pokers, sunflowers, green cestrum and yellow-green 'Limelight' roses. It is important to make this kind of arrangement look loose and flowing rather than stiff and upright.

Here an old milk jug contains cream gladioli, 'Pascali' roses, branches of green oranges, perennial aster and dangling green amaranthus.

Wedding flowers at Hughes Park in the Clare Valley of South Australia. A superb old épergne was used with pink grasses, cascading stems of fairy bells (*Dierama pendulum*), 'Pascali' and 'Eiffel Tower' roses, and green fern.

A wedding arrangement in my cast-iron blacksmith container, this time using gladioli, the roses 'Carina', 'Eiffel Tower' and 'Shell Queen' (a pale sport of 'Queen Elizabeth') and silvery statice. This was placed in the entrance hall.

One of two identical arrangements decorating the entrance to a marquee for a country wedding in early spring. Bronze and olive urns hold long branches of wild pear blossom, spiraea, white bearded iris, arum lilies, long stems of single white *Rosa laevigata* and drooping sprays of white broom, *Genista monosperma pendula*.

South Australian Rose Society Special Shows

Each spring and autumn the South Australian Rose Society holds a special rose show at which the different branches of the society are invited to arrange displays.

Rose Society Spring Show 2002

The Chaffey Rose Club branch, from Renmark, and the Riverina group from Hay, put together this striking display for the spring Rose Society show in October 2002. Here masses of roses, strelitzias, palm spathes and fasciated ash are used with sheep made of tin in a very large exhibit symbolising rural Australia.

A rustic cart filled with 'Fred Howard' roses formed another part of the display.

(*Left*) Another view of the Chaffey Rose Club display, showing a pedestal using palm spathes and strelitzia, with 'Baccara' and 'Gold Medal' roses cascading downwards to the sheep at the base. Yellow iris and roses snuggle into a bale of straw on the left and an ingenious floor arrangement of gold roses using a curled palm spathe as a container sits in the background

The container in this section of the Chaffey Rose Club display is covered with melaleuca bark. A huge wash-up bowl filled with oasis hides inside. It contains a palm spathe showing its flower head, loops of *Asparagus horridus*, fasciated ash and a twisted wisteria branch. Flowers include pokers, blue iris and 'Just Joey' roses. Much of this material came from Hay in New South Wales, 750 kilometres from Renmark. The containers and flowers were collected from Renmark on the way through. It took some packing!

Rose Society Spring Show 1995

For the spring Rose Society Show in the Adelaide Town Hall in 1995 my task was to organise Flemish flower arrangements in front of a background of lovely old oak panelling. I brought my antique containers, pedestals and flowers in two vans. Huge black urns on massive plinths weighed 40 kilograms – it was quite a feat getting them into the Town Hall.

A view of the two black urn displays. Note the cut watermelon at the base of the right plinth, and the pineapple and rockmelons on the top of the plinth, to bring the line down from high on the left to low on the right.

A large urn holding the copper-coloured roses 'Vienna Charm', 'Brandy', 'Pierre B' and 'Copper Gem', arranged formally against a pillar. The lush green rose foliage shows up as a background to each bloom. I must say that my favourite colour scheme is apricot with bronze foliage.

Rose Society Autumn Show 2006

As part of a display for the Adelaide Rose Society's autumn show in 2006 I featured a large basket on a pedestal, using masses of green-yellow *Kniphofia ensifolia* – I love the green tips. The roses filling in the arrangement are 'Gold Medal', 'Graham Thomas' and 'Diamond Jubilee', all looking paler than I expected. The apricot and yellow colourings are intensified by the use of the purple foliage of *Prunus nigra*.

Rose Society Autumn Show 2009

In autumn 2009 I put together a massed display for two country groups, the local Chaffey Rose Branch of which I am the patron, and the South East Branch of South Australia. Brian Wagner from the

An overview of the colour blending that was carried out in lovely old containers, and using pedestals of varying heights.

A simple massed pedestal arrangement of 'Christian Dior' roses. This rose can hold its form for over a week in cool weather.

A large pedestal of kniphofias, goldenrod, pomegranates, 'Baccara' roses and yellow tansy to bring yellow through the focal area. Autumn foliage of glory vine and purple prunus ties in with the grapes and pomegranates at the base to give that 'season of mists and mellow fruitfulness' look.

My two spelter ewers hold ornamental pear branches laden with brown berries, coupled with pink and cream 'American Heritage' roses along with 'Helena', the soft apricot-yellow sport of 'Helen Traubel' in the lower ewer.

A small ewer holding the soft yellow 'Helena', the sport of 'Helen Traubel' that occurred in Treloar's nursery in 1982. It is used here with rose hips.

South East provided huge bunches of Delbard roses from his nursery to add variety.

Delbard from France has given us some stunning striped roses in the last ten years. He has also won many awards for perfume. Scent in roses is now analysed in the same way as in perfumes and in the bouquet of wines. There can be touches of many aromas in all of them. In roses, damask, lemon, orange, moss, tea and forest oak are just a few. Here blooms of the long-lasting 'Chardon Rosier', a popular Delbard rose, are arranged with rose hips, crab-apples and a few medlars on skewers.

Rose Society of Victoria 1995

The Rose Society of Victoria put on a huge display at David Jones in Collins Street, Melbourne, in 1995. Barry Johnson, Trevor Grant and I, with many helpers, arranged large bowls of roses which were held aloft by life-size Grecian goddesses. The effect reflected in the glass mirrors was magic. There were areas of red, pink, mauve, white, cream, yellow and apricot roses throughout the ground floor. All the roses came with me by plane from Renmark.

'Sonia' roses are teamed with grey eucalypt leaves.

Part of the yellow section – 'Graham Thomas' mixed with 'Matterhorn' on the left and 'Buccaneer' with rose hips on the right.

Iris Convention, Adelaide 2002

I love irises, a great flower that combines so well with roses in arrangements.

Demonstrating at an Iris Convention in Adelaide, I used two modern pottery containers into which I placed loops of fasciated ash and apricot iris. At the base are containers already completed, which were inadvertently placed with their backs on view. I was appalled when I noticed this afterwards and quickly remedied the situation!

New Zealand 2008

In November 2008 I led a bus tour of New Zealand gardens which was organised by the Illawarra Rose Society of New South Wales. I stayed on in the South Island for the annual Timaru Rose Festival, whose theme that year was 'Flowers in History'. I was asked to demonstrate flower arranging from the sixteenth to the early twentieth century.

A garland showing how small flowers like cornflowers, forget-me-nots, anchusa and gentians can give that touch of blue to the pale pink and white roses, penstemons and lilies. This arrangement represents those of Jesuit priest Daniel Seghers, who worked in the second half of the sixteenth century. He often used roses with thistles and thorny plant material as symbols of good and evil.

A trug basket contains a horizontal line of grouped blue delphiniums and pink foxgloves with a centre of huge pink peonies. The foxgloves had very long stems and it seemed a sacrilege to cut them off. By next morning the horizontal tips had turned upwards which made the whole arrangement look more natural. I placed the arrangement, celebrating the early twentieth century, on a low dropside table.

A mixture of flowers in the style of Jan Van Huysum (1682–1749) who always used white lilies, orange and blue flowers and often sunflowers, sometimes turned side-on to show their profile. Here we have the Austrian copper rose, '*Rosa foetida bicolor*', tulips cascading downwards to show the poise of the flower on the stem, opium poppies, campanulas, delphiniums, lupins for a touch of blue, and 'Rose de Rescht'. Van Huysum used white flowers through his arrangements to give impact when viewed from a distance. Notice also the impact of the two 'Rembrandt' red bearded iris.

(*Left*) There were lots of blue delphiniums and mixed red roses left at the end of the demonstration and so I tried a red and blue combination which I feel succeeded. Blue is a difficult colour in poor light as it recedes and loses impact, but here it looks good.

I took along five containers on my trip to New Zealand, one of them my silver tea urn. I placed the lid at the base as an accessory and used delphiniums, iris, cornflowers, the bourbon rose 'Paul Ricault', salvia, foxgloves, watsonias and hollyhocks, all picked from local gardens. Soft colours were very popular in paintings in France during the reigns of Louis XIV and Louis XV in the late seventeenth and early eighteenth century, when the French court was at the height of its glory.

(Photograph courtesy James Manifold)

Tasmanian Heritage Rose Society 2009

At a demonstration in Campbell Town, Tasmania for a meeting of Heritage Rose Society members, many local gardeners brought in lovely flowers for me to use.

A curve-legged pedestal is ideal for a mass of curvaceous opium poppies, foxgloves, lupins, roses and palest pink peonies. The stems of the poppies were held under a flame to seal the ends. They gave that important flow downwards, showing the beautiful grey green foliage.

An old, blackened cast-iron cooking pot contains an assortment of mauve roses, daisies, foxgloves, peonies, love-in-the-mist and watsonias in pastel colours with dark purple bearded and Siberian iris and lupins to tie in with the dark colour of the pot. Fortunately I had acquired ten stems of peonies from a peony farm a couple of days before and they had opened up nicely for the occasion.

National Rose Society, Kiama, New South Wales 2009

(*Right*) At a meeting of the National Rose Society in Kiama, New South Wales, two vertical tin containers filled with lovely loops of prickly *Asparagus horridus* and silver *Adenanthos sericea* were used with pale pink 'Royal Highness', 'Grand Siècle' and deep pink 'Peter Frankenfeld'. The dark drape gave weight to the the base of the arrangement.

I used my boat-shaped woven container at Kiama to hold an 'underwater' style of arrangement. Driftwood is the feature with grouped watsonias, the mauve roses 'Lagerfeld', 'Blue Moon' and 'Lady X', with deep magenta Austin 'Sophy's Rose', combined with globe artichokes, echeveria succulents and ornamental kale.

Barn Palais, Mount Gambier 2010

The Barn Palais in Mount Gambier includes a convention centre that can hold 800 people, a restaurant, beautiful motel units, and a

A huge old urn with lovely handles holds a ten-litre bucket containing a large block of oasis. There are group placings of alstroemeria, yellow and brown sunflowers with some of their seedpods giving extra interest, sprays of *Rosa woodsii fendleri*, pokers, variegated tulips, purple grapes and an artichoke. The roses are 'Anne Marie Trechslin' and 'Camille Pisarro'. Quinces and pomegranates give weight to the base.

Two copper containers from Japan hold a duo arrangement of Delbard's striped roses in groups with rose hips and grapes. Loops of defoliated glory vine join the two parts together and give depth. Pokers tie in with the colour scheme.

large garden of historic old trees, roses, perennials and bulbs grown to perfection in rich volcanic acid soil – a gardener's paradise. In March 2010 the garden was open as part of Australia's Open Garden Scheme, with proceeds going towards the David Ruston Sculpture Appeal. The brilliant young flower arranger Danny Hoffmann and I enjoyed demonstrating twice over the weekend.

A cast-iron figurine displays a flowing design of soft colours. Blue iris, asters in pink and white, silver eucalypt and cypress branches are combined with deep pink 'Peter Frankenfeld' and soft mauve 'Lagerfeld' roses. Dangling amaranthus brings the deep colour through the design.

A cascading crescent of Manchurian pear with its small brown fruit and rich green foliage ties in well with the colour of the container. The roses are the David Austin variety, 'Evelyn'.

Renmark 2010

In 2006 a life-long friend of my family, Mrs Merridy Howie, suggested that a sculpture be erected in Renmark honouring my life with flowers. This idea was taken up by a committee who chose a modern metal and bronze structure depicting me, with secateurs in hand, peering through a trellis of roses with a background of selected flowers featuring the curves and swirls of sculptural pods and leaves.

For our Renmark Christmas Pageant 2009 I was seated on a chair in front of a maquette of the proposed sculpture, surrounded by baskets of apricot and yellow roses. A car towed the low trailer along the main street.

The unveiling of the sculpture on 16 October 2010 was one of the most memorable days of my life. A large crowd was in attendance. Mr Kelvin Trimper, Chairman of the Sculpture Committee, introduced the proceedings brilliantly and Mrs Sheenagh Harris, President of the World Federation of Rose Societies, performed the unveiling in her inimitable way. A special dinner that evening in the new dining room at the Ruston Rose Centre left me quite speechless. Although Dr Tommy Cairns, a past President of the World Federation of Rose Societies, was unable to be present, he gave the keynote speech through a DVD and pointed out my past activities with great panache. Several times I was worried that he might mention some of my weaknesses, of which there are many. Fortunately there were only very subtle hints, recognised by my closest friends. Again, a night with memories I will cherish forever.

Along with this extraordinary honour, several other awards have a special significance for me. The Dean Hole Medal from the Royal National Rose Society, the Gold Medal of the World Federation of Rose Societies and the biggest surprise of all, joining the Baroness Lily de Gerlache de Gomery as a President Emeritus of the World Federation of Rose Societies. I have certainly been a very lucky man.

Responding to the unveiling, watched by Kelvin Trimper.
(Photograph courtesy Marjorie Todd)

A general crowd scene after the unveiling.

Chapter 4

The World of Rose Conferences

The World Rose Conventions I have attended over the years have given me a great deal of pleasure. I have formed many lasting friendships with people of similar interests from around the world. I have also learnt much from the excellent speakers, been stimulated and excited by the quality of the rose shows, while the beautiful and frequently exotic gardens I have visited have been a joy and delight.

London 1968

(Condensed from an article published in *The Australian Rose Annual*, 1969, page 63.)

The International Rose Conference in London in 1968 saw a new organisation come into being. During the conference the World Federation of Rose Societies was established through the initiative of the Baroness Lily de Gerlache de Gomery, President of the Belgian Rose Society. Fifteen countries became members of the World Federation, and it was decided to hold a World Convention every three years, beginning in 1971.

Overseas delegates to the 1968 London conference met the Queen Mother, Patron of the Royal National Rose Society, at an afternoon reception at St James's Palace. Dr Alfred Thomas from Melbourne and I were the two Australians fortunate enough to be at the reception. (I met the Queen Mother on two subsequent occasions. In 1976, again in St James's Palace, she was present as part of 'Rosescent'. But best of all, when I gave Peter Beales and staff a bit of a hand with staging at the Royal Sandringham Show, the Queen Mother arrived with her grandson Prince Charles. I remember Her Majesty wore palest apricot with matching accessories, and pale pink and soft mauve on the other two occasions. The Queen Mother had a wonderful way of giving you her complete attention, then that lovely smile which meant that your time was up.)

The 1968 conference began with the usual rose show. Before leaving home I optimistically arranged for a box of roses and hips to be air-freighted to London, as my garden in Renmark had enjoyed a wonderful early winter flush of blooms. Good friends, Eric and Myrtle Trimper, sent them off and they arrived in good condition despite the 30-hour flight. The cultivars were mostly yellows and golds, which I thought would hold their colour best during the long journey. I recut the stems, put them in boiling water and then into cool water for the night. Next day they were just right for arranging, which was 110 hours and 12,000 miles after they were picked! The roses were used in a class for a pedestal arrangement and they were lucky enough to receive a third prize.

Julia Clements, world-famous floral artist and judge, said of my entry, as reported in *The Rose Annual* 1969 (page 169):

> Another exciting exhibit in the class was staged by David Ruston of South Australia, who made a huge display of lovely copper-coloured roses brought from Australia, set in a copper tea urn that he bought in London. This was much admired, although we in England could not appreciate the fact that Australians do not seem to make their roses flow out at the back for a pedestal group, theirs being flat.

It was the first time that roses from Australia had been shown in England and they caused quite a sensation.

The great Summer Rose Show was a magnificent spectacle of roses. There were at least twenty-five trade exhibits, some 60 feet (19 m) long and 10 feet (3 m) high – a solid wall of flowers. There was so much to see that I was there for eleven hours. Even at closing time I would have been happy to keep on looking at the exhibits, which must have covered several acres.

When the show was over, during the Rose Conference, I re-used the copper tea urn at a joint demonstration with Julia Clements from England and the Baroness Lily de Gerlache de Gomery from Belgium. I used all 'Fragrant Cloud' roses bred by Tantau.

London Rose Conference 1968: 'Fragrant Cloud' roses arranged in a copper tea urn.

Lectures were delivered over two days at the Hilton Hotel in London and Brigadier Lucas Phillips, Jack Harkness and I were to speak on 'Informal Gardening with Roses'. I compared the growth habits of roses in the different growing conditions around the world, and discussed the attractive effect of massed, tiered planting in borders and the importance of colour blending; Brigadier Phillips spoke about the changing trends in companion planting and the importance of choosing the right plant for the area into which it is to go; Jack Harkness described the way in which climbers could be used throughout the garden, extolling, in particular, the virtues of the vast array of wichurana roses and the attractions of placing climbers on a pillar.

The conference could truly be called international, as there were speakers from many countries talking about such topics as climates, understocks, cultivars, hybridising and general culture. The grand finale came with a magnificent banquet which ended an unforgettable experience and great fellowship of rosarians from all parts of the world.

Hamilton, New Zealand 1971

In 1971, Hamilton in New Zealand held the first World Federation of Rose Societies Convention. Forty years on, this show still rates as one of the best ever, with an enormous rose show, wonderful flower arrangements and tours to many superb rose gardens.

I decided to enter the most difficult class in the show open to rose clubs or individuals, for nine bunches of roses, with six stems in each bunch, a total of fifty-four stems. I managed to win a second prize after being held up for four hours in quarantine in Auckland while they searched for pests and diseases.

Much to my disappointment I missed the following convention, in Chicago in 1974, because of a flood threat from the River Darling – which did not eventuate.

London/Oxford 1976

In July 1976 London and Oxford hosted a monumental event called 'Rosescent' to celebrate the centenary of the Royal National Rose Society, founded in 1876 by the then Dean of Rochester Cathedral and prolific writer on the rose, Dean Reynolds Hole. This was the first rose society in the world.

The first event I attended was the Great Summer Show, held in the Royal Horticultural Halls in Westminster, in London, during the hottest and driest year on record in England. The halls had glass panels in the roof to let in natural light and were very hot indeed, so hot that roses like 'Red Devil' started to burn at the edges. This can happen in Australia but very seldom does it occur in England.

Australia was one of the countries, along with Europe, the United Kingdom, Asia, countries of the Near East, South Africa, North America and New Zealand, who staged a non-competitive display around an octagon draped in pale blue material, each section 2.3 metres wide and 2.6 metres high. Victorians May Pask and Lois Barnett, and I, used orange, red and yellow roses for massed work to create 'A Sunburnt Country' and with this in mind I brought along the rose bush 'Eiffel Tower', complete with roots, branches and thorns to use with 'Julia's Rose' for 'down under'. The rose bush was placed upside down! We used yellow, orange and red roses and hips to enrich the massed arrangements – one a pedestal arrangement with a hidden container (a wash-up bowl), and the second an arrangement on a pedestal using a lovely copper samovar I found in Bath.

From London there were tours to Hidcote Manor, Blenheim Palace, day visits to the Cotswolds, to Bath and the Royal Horticultural Society Garden at Wisley, which contains a huge number of species roses and has, I think, the most comprehensive botanical and gardening bookshop in the world.

We proceeded by bus to Oxford for the rest of the conference, staying in student accommodation during the summer break. Lectures were of the highest standard with such eminent speakers as Dr Gerard Krussman of Germany, Ralph Moore of the United States and Jack Harkness, Graham Thomas and Edward Le Grice, all from the United Kingdom.

I also demonstrated. Lois Barnett from Victoria described this in *The Australian Rose Annual* 1977 (page 151):

Mr Ruston's theatre, where he demonstrated, was filled to overflowing. Every seat was occupied – all the stairs were filled with seated figures, all the standing room at the back was filled with a curious and enthusiastic audience. Mr Ruston showed experience and skilful handling of roses, material and colour blending, giving each arrangement an informal distinction, such as the tall pewter stand supporting a silver dish which was the perfect container for the beautifully arranged 'Blue Moon' roses against an asymmetrical background of silvery grey

The side of the octagon showing Australia's display. Note the central exhibit of the rose 'down under'.

gum with deep purple roses cleverly placed to offset the subtle line of deep pink roses – a perfect colour harmony. He showed versatility too when using two or three roses very cleverly with interesting material in very modern containers. Mr Ruston was bombarded with questions at the end of this brilliant demonstration and those present learnt a great deal about choosing and arranging roses. Congratulations to a fine Australian ambassador.

Visits around Oxford were to Stratford-on-Avon, Mottisfont Abbey, Bone Hill at St Albans, Windsor Castle and gardens, Saville Gardens and Queen Mary's Garden in Regents Park. We also attended the Royal Horticultural Show at Stoneleigh House and Hatfield House, home of that great gardener, the Marchioness of Salisbury. What more could anyone wish for – a great combination of roses, historic homes and gardens!

Pretoria 1979

Pretoria hosted the World Convention in 1979 and this was very enjoyable, with superb roses, huge gardens and excellent lectures topped off with a four-day safari which included a trip at night with an orange moon glowing above. We were amazed at the beauty of the numerous rose gardens we visited in the Rand, the Cape provinces and Durban. The convention was very ably organised by Jack and Mary Wise. Their daughter, Sheenagh Harris, is the present World Federation of Rose Societies President (2009–2012). South Africa will again host the World Convention in 2012 with Sheenagh at the helm.

Jerusalem 1981

Jerusalem, in 1981, had as its theme 'Rose Pilgrimage'. This most interesting conference, held in a very hot, dry land, was of great benefit for those of us living in similar conditions. It has been one of only two conferences of the WFRS held in autumn, a perfect time for good blooms after the end of the summer heat. The conference was held in the Hilton Hotel which looked a little incongruous rising high above the ancient city. Intriguing exhibitions included 'Flora in our Biblical Heritage', 'The Rose in Philately', 'The Rose in Art' and 'Roses in History'.

One of the best speakers was Jack Harkness, a great author on roses in the twentieth century. Jack gave a dramatic talk on his breeding with *Hulthemia persica* (now *Rosa persica*), a rose from arid areas in Iran – single yellow flowers with a brilliant red blotch in the centre.

Ancient Jerusalem was fascinating with its narrow winding streets, old churches, tiny shops packed with curios of brass, silver, wood and bronze, and people from all races and religions. A highlight for me was the Garden of Gethsemane with its 2000-year-old olives with their old gnarled butts and tortured branches. A trip to the Black Sea and ancient Jericho made us realise how ancient is the civilisation of the region.

Baden-Baden 1983

The 1983 Convention in the old German city of Baden-Baden was fantastic. The food at the banquet was served at each table from a train that meandered around the room. The Baden-Baden rose trial ground was one of the most beautiful in the world, with the gold medal going to 'Julia's Rose' because of its unique colour. It is interesting to find that tens of thousands of 'Julia's Rose' bushes are grown in Australia for the cut flower trade since it was carried by Kate Ceberano in her wedding bouquet. At a dinner for special guests the wild strawberries from the Black Forest proved much sweeter that the huge modern varieties. Baden-Baden is a casino city and the gamblers were very obvious as they did not appear until the afternoon of each day.

Toronto 1985

In 1985 it was Toronto's turn – again, beautiful gardens, lots of species roses, fantastic peonies and an excellent rose show with lots of support from American rosarians. Over 600 people attended the conference, coming from twenty-three different countries.

Lectures were held over three days. A highlight for me was the lecture given by Dr Toru Onodera from Japan who spoke on 'Rose Planting as Bonsai'. He showed slides of roses growing on rocks and tree stumps showing gnarled roots but flowering with the utmost freedom. Another great speaker was David Gilad, formerly World President and also convenor of the Jerusalem Convention but now with the Meilland Company. David spoke of a whole new class of roses to be called 'Meidiland Roses' – hardy, disease free, no pruning required and flowering freely from ground level upwards. (We have since found that they need drastic pruning every five years to prevent them from becoming woody).

For my flower demonstration I was offered roses from a Canadian friend whose precious bushes had to be covered with leaves and straw to a depth of 18 inches (45 cm) for protection against cold each winter. Even then they died back to nearly ground level. I went picking, and by the time I had cut the second long stem my hostess had to go inside for a Scotch! I got the message. I then chose lots of flowering shrubs and foliage, and it seemed that my demonstration would have only two rose stems. But back at the hotel I found a huge bowl of glass-house 'Samantha' roses, five days old, which I was given permission to use. Then I discovered a young member of staff polishing forty huge silver tea urns, and asked if I could borrow one. He looked somewhat amazed but handed one over. Everyone said that my subsequent arrangements and demonstration were magnificent considering the circumstances.

Sydney 1988

Early in 1986 Heather Rumsey wrote to me asking if I would convene the rose display for the World Rose Convention to be held at Sydney University in April 1988 – the year of Australia's bicentenary. After giving the matter a great deal of thought I decided to tackle the job. The worst obstacle was distance – over 1100 kilometres. After two trips to Sydney to look at the venue, we decided that I would try to fill the long unbroken wall of the University Refectory with a display of roses from my own garden. We would ask the six state rose societies to fill the other long wall (broken up by arched windows), while Heather Rumsey would convene a nurserymen's display down the centre of the hall.

The cedar panelling and the wonderful mural above it would provide a magnificent backdrop to the display. We decided to use pedestals and low tables against the panelling. With such a lovely background the next problem was the choice of containers. My collection of antique vases was the obvious choice, but this presented problems of transport. I decided to take the risk of sending them by freight in twelve large crates. We packed them carefully so they could not move in transit and they went off to Sydney over Easter, a week before the event.

'200 Years of Roses' seemed an apt title for our bicentennial year. I realised that this would have been much easier to do in spring than autumn, but I hoped there would be enough tea roses, bourbons and noisettes available for the early period. I started summer pruning nine weeks before the show and continued for six weeks to ensure that there would be plenty of roses whatever the weather. I worked in six tonnes of mineral mix over a period of four weeks. The first flush appeared in five weeks on the earliest pruned bushes.

We started picking on Thursday 7 April and six of us picked all day, labelling each variety with the name and date of introduction. I kept on finding more varieties until by nightfall we had 150 varieties ready for refrigeration overnight and packing the next day, as well as a lot of apricot and orange roses, foliage, hips and berries for the decoration of the Great Hall for the opening ceremony. We packed all Friday morning and then a lad drove me 240 kilometres to Adelaide Airport with twenty-five boxes of roses. We had booked these in with Ansett Airlines weeks in advance, only to be told on arrival that the plane was full and only ten boxes could be taken on my flight. The rest would go on a later flight via Melbourne. The plane was late leaving because of heavy rain in Sydney and when I eventually arrived I found the taxi truck had got tired of waiting and left. After a great deal of effort I managed to get the ten boxes to Sydney University, where Rose Society of South Australia members had unpacked the flower vases and filled sixty buckets ready for the mammoth task of getting 6000 stems cut, sorted in order of year of introduction, put in water and then carted downstairs to two cool rooms for storage from Friday night until Sunday evening.

I went back to the airport to pick up the other fifteen boxes where the Ansett staff finally told me that they had been off-loaded in Melbourne and would not arrive until next day. The roses finally arrived at one o'clock the next afternoon, twenty hours after they had been booked in at Adelaide for a one and a half hour flight. However, to be fair to Ansett Airlines, they *did* carry something like 500 kilograms of flowers from Adelaide to Sydney free of charge.

On Monday a further eight boxes arrived for my floral demonstration, six boxes on Tuesday for the decorations for the banquet and four boxes on Wednesday for baskets to decorate the Hall of Fame. The South Australian Rose Society was an invaluable help, as was an international group of volunteers who helped with the arrangements, all to be done in chronological order and stretching for 25 metres along the wall of the Refectory – a huge task When it was

(*Above and right*) Two sections of the finished display in the University Refectory.

A concealed wash-up basin holds a mass of red 'Baccara', yellow 'Golden Giant' and apricot 'Thais' roses with long sprays of 'Rambling Rector' hips and green Ohanez grapes.

Eric Trimper's huge bowl of 300 stems of 'Baccara'. In the 1989 *Australian Rose Annual* I was given the credit for this arrangement – which Eric has never let me forget! The reverse occurred when Eric helped me with a demonstration for the twenty-fifth birthday of the Gawler Flower Group. At the end, the vote of thanks was given to Eric. I missed out!

finally completed after four hours, it looked magnificent against the beautiful oak panelling. Eric Trimper had retrieved a *Women's Weekly* trophy which had been in storage for twenty years and used it to house 300 stems of 'Baccara' roses. This bowl became the centrepiece of the display of over a hundred arrangements in my antique containers.

Belfast 1991

Northern Ireland was next in 1991. From the very start, when masses of lovely flower displays welcomed us at Belfast Airport, it was non-stop entertainment all the way, with wonderful roses, fine food, Irish wit, and great hospitality. The Irish night at the Europa Hotel, the Gala Concert at Elmwood Hall with all items having a rosy theme, the Rose Emerald Gala Banquet and the final closing ceremony were all very memorable.

The lectures were as diverse as they were interesting. Pat Dickson's opening lecture, 'The Rose Men of Ulster', was given to a packed house and made us all realise what a great debt we owe to the firms of Dickson and McGredy over a period of nearly a hundred years.

One of the most brilliant speakers I have ever heard was Dr Charles Nelson – erudite, witty and charming. He is the taxonomist at the Glasnevin Botanic Gardens in Dublin. His topic was 'The History of the Rose in Ireland' and he held us spellbound while he traced the history of roses from the simple native forms, to Thomas Moore's 'last rose of the summer', reputed to be 'Old Blush', to some of the roses like 'Souvenir de St Anne's', a semi-double sport of 'Souvenir de la Malmaison', which was found in Ireland.

James Burnside, one of the group of Northern Irish flower arrangers responsible for the lavish and extremely beautiful displays in all the major venues of the Conference, gave a wonderful demonstration of a summer miscellany in a marquee at Lady Dixon Park – the best rose garden I saw on my travels and one of the best demonstrations I have seen anywhere.

This was followed by a trip to Eire where we saw superb gardens warmed by the influence of the Gulf Stream – and well watered from above.

Christchurch 1994

The 1994 Christchurch Convention was very special to me as I was World President from 1991 to 1994. The best displays of flower arranging that I have ever seen were at this convention, all set out in an enormous marquee. Two huge refrigerated trucks holding hundreds of buckets of flowers made my demonstrating very easy, with peonies, delphiniums, foxgloves and lupins available, all with very long stems. I was asked to do a 'World President's Welcome' display using huge urns on pedestals all containing massive arrangements of peonies, roses, foxgloves, watsonias and polygonatum (Solomon's seal).

A special moment for me in Christchurch welcoming delegates to the Conference.

(*Right*) Some of my arrangements featured in the 'welcome' display at the entrance to the flower arrangement marquee.

A design of larkspurs, delphiniums, foxgloves, stocks, daylilies, red peonies and roses with various types of foliage.

(*Right*) I used my samovar to house a Flemish arrangement of iris, lupins, lilies, species gladioli, delphiniums and roses 'Complicata', 'Rose de Rescht' and 'Koenigin von Danemarck' together with lemons, which tie in with the fruit on the base. The lid and bird's nest act as accessories. Red iris and lupins give the rich colour loved by Rembrandt in his portraiture.

I was also asked to demonstrate and I managed seven arrangements in just over an hour! All the flowers I used were grown in local gardens.

Again, garden visits were great fun with lots of colour-blended opium poppies toning with the old roses. In one garden all the poppy seed heads were stolen the night after we visited. I hope it wasn't one of us!

After this superb conference with an attendance of over 1100, it was

off to the old French settlement of Akaroa nestling in a sheltered bay on the Banks Peninsula. I was guest of garden writer, the indomitable Barbara Lea Taylor. She wrote up the demonstration I did there, calling me irreverently Australian', and said that I 'demonstrated at the speed of light'!

Benelux 1997

Belgium, Holland and Luxembourg were co-hosts for the 1997 Benelux Convention. Again, a magic display in the ancient Town Hall, beautiful rose gardens, lovely parks and meeting gracious Queen Paola, made this conference one of the highlights of my life with roses. It was here that I had the pleasure of demonstrating flower arranging in the old coach house at Hex Castle, home of the Comte d'Ursel, in Liege. Hex Castle was built in the eighteenth century by the bishops of Liege. The coach house was filled with ornate old horse-drawn carriages dating back to the time the castle was built. It made a very picturesque backdrop to the arrangements. The magnificent garden with its huge collection of species roses, with ancient varieties of not only roses, but also vegetables and fruit trees, ensured that it was awarded the bronze plaque of the World Federation of Rose Societies for a garden of historic significance.

A Flemish arrangement where an old copper pot contains sunflowers turned towards the back, lilies, pale peonies, iris, anchusa for the touch of blue, and scabious. The collection of fruit at the base along with a bird's nest is reminiscent of paintings from the eighteenth century.

Houston 2000

The year 2000 was the turn of Houston, Texas. They hosted a big rose show with excellent lectures and demonstrations, lots of gardens large and small and a visit to Shreveport, headquarters of the American Rose Society. On visits to private rose gardens in Houston I was amazed how hard some of the exhibitors pruned their roses to get huge blooms. Sometimes only three or four shoots were left per plant and these were disbudded to one bloom per stem. This greatly reduced their garden display. Also, sliding screens were used on roofs and fences for protection from the elements. Exhibiting in the United States is taken very seriously and the results are amazing.

We were baffled that most major American rose shows are not open to the general public, whereas in Australia, New Zealand, South Africa and Europe thousands attend such events and this is a great help in allaying costs and enrolling new members. I was most impressed that exhibitors came from all over America with superb roses in all classes for both spring and autumn (or should I say, fall?) shows. One class I loved was the Dorothy Stemler Award for a container of old garden roses with entries from five states. The old roses were some of the best I have ever seen. I have a feeling that they were all disbudded! I also found when driving about that very few front gardens had any

Also at Hex, hollyhocks, iris, peonies, tulips, calendulas, delphiniums, old roses, antirrhinums and tuberoses are placed in a terracotta urn with fruit at the base.

roses. It was all lawns and evergreens, so different from Australia where there are roses everywhere.

I missed Glasgow in 2003 because of a health problem but heard good reports of lovely public rose gardens and great hospitality.

Osaka 2006

Osaka in Japan in 2006 was superbly organised and magic from start to finish – one of the best conferences ever with immaculate lush healthy rose gardens and huge public gardens of 30 000 – 40 000 rose bushes. At the beginning, because of the late season, roses were in short supply, but at the end they were at their best. The country was lush with rice fields everywhere and beautiful forests of both deciduous and evergreen trees – different species for the different altitudes. The peonies in the Jindai Botanic Gardens were in full voluptuous bloom, as was the rose garden specialising in 1950–1980 hybrid teas and floribundas. They were more colourful and plentiful than more modern varieties. This rose garden was awarded a bronze plaque by the World Federation of Rose Societies which was presented at the Vancouver conference in 2009. The trip to Gifu was a great experience but being in the hills at a higher altitude, only species, teas and early climbers were out. But we could all imagine the display that would be forthcoming in a week or two. Gifu is the largest and greatest rose garden in the world – a commercial enterprise that attracts 40 000 visitors a day during the spring and autumn flushes. I will be returning to Gifu after the Heritage Rose Conference which will be held at Sakura, near Tokyo, in 2011. It should be perfect timing, being fourteen days later than Osaka.

Adelaide 2008

In October 2008 Adelaide hosted a World Federation of Rose Societies Regional Convention as part of the South Australian Rose Society's centenary celebrations. Over 300 participants from all over the world gathered in the city of churches to enjoy an excellent programme of lectures, garden visits and the centenary rose show.

The conference was extremely well organised with brilliant lectures from both overseas and Australian experts. The overseas speakers included Tommy Cairns (USA), Dr Gerard Meyland (Switzerland), Alain Meilland (France), Keith Zary (USA) and Thomas Proll (Germany). There were tours to the Fleurieu Peninsula and to the Barossa and Clare Valleys and Renmark, which gave overseas visitors a taste of the outback with a shearing demonstration, a visit to wetlands along the Murray at Banrock Station and accommodation overlooking a bend in the Murray River at Renmark. Those from very cold climates were amazed at the size of the tea roses, Chinas and noisettes and the enormous mounds of banksia roses, 'Mermaid', *Rosa bracteata*, *R. laevigata* and *R. fortuneana*, all of which love hot conditions.

At the rose show in the centre of the hall to celebrate the centenary of the Rose Society of South Australia I produced a display featuring roses bred in the past hundred years. A pedestal housing roses from 1983–2008 was the centrepiece while three large pots at the base contained roses from each of the other 25-year periods. The arrangement from 1908–1933 had to rely on tea roses but the other periods contained hybrid teas. This included such wonderful old varieties as 'Mr Lincoln', 'Sonia', 'Ophelia' and her sports, 'Columbia' and its sports, 'Comtesse Vandal', 'Crimson Glory' and, of course, 'Peace'. All the roses were named on a card at the base and were grouped to give extra impact. Blue delphiniums were used to give height and iris, guelder rose, phlomis, salvia and cornflowers gave that touch of blue and white that combines well with any colour. White weeping broom cascaded downwards. The pedestal was of fibreglass and so much easier to handle than a genuine stone one.

The centenary display showing roses from 1908 to 2008.

Vancouver 2009

The fifteenth International Rose Conference was held in June 2009 in the lovely city of Vancouver – a city of huge parks and gardens, surrounded by forests and mountains.

The rose show in the new city hall, which is covered with a green mossy roof, was very well presented. Exhibitors came from all over Canada and the United States. I particularly enjoyed the well-filled classes for old roses – those that can withstand intense winter cold. Gallicas, mosses and albas were all spectacular and the glass vases with old roses and companion plants like delphiniums, foxgloves and campanulas were stunning. The exhibition roses were also huge and the grand champion was called 'Tekome', perfectly formed, very pale pink, gaining more points than any rose I have ever seen. It was staged by Teizo

A simple arrangement using the lovely buds of 'Princess Margaret of England'.

(Photograph courtesy James Manifold)

Yoshike of Japan. Local florists put on a magic display of glass-house roses grouped in big, bold bunches with other dramatic material set off perfectly with a creamy gauze curtain hanging on each side.

Lectures were again of the highest quality. It was encouraging to find that of the twenty-two presentations, eleven dealt with heritage roses! This demonstrates that lovers of both old and modern roses are working together much more cooperatively.

Canadian speakers were Brad Jalburt on 'Modern Roses for the Pacific Area', Claire Laberge from the Montreal Botanical Gardens on 'Species Roses in the Landscape', Alec Globe on 'The History of the Rose in Canada' and Patrick White, who gave 'A Tribute to Felicitas Svejda', talking about the sub-zero roses she had bred using *Rosa rugosa* as one parent. Svejda's work has provided many repeat-flowering shrub roses for cold climates.

Helga Brichet from Umbria in Italy traced the importance of the repeat-flowering China roses from Asia combining with the once-blooming roses of Europe and America to produce the long-flowering roses of today.

A highlight for me was the lecture given by Sheenagh Harris, President of the World Federation of Rose Societies, on the 120 roses named after English royalty, from the crowning of Queen Victoria in 1840 onwards. Sheenagh had been unable to photograph a bush of 'Princess Margaret of England', bred by Meilland in 1969, so when I got home I picked some flowers, put them in an urn – a copy of a Medici sixteenth-century one – and sent her the photograph which appears opposite.

Sandton 2012

The next WFRS World Rose Convention is to be held in Sandton, near Johannesburg, in October 2012. South Africa has superb gardens with a large climatic range, and produces a lot of cut roses for the European market. There will be a safari in a game reserve and a conducted tour of gardens from Bloemfontein to Cape Town, and along the garden route from Cape Town to Port Elizabeth and Durban. We will also visit the small town of Bedford which contains all the roses mentioned in Gwen Fagan's classic book, *Roses at the Cape of Good Hope* (1988).

Chapter 5

The World of Heritage Roses

As much as I like modern roses, my real passion is for older varieties. Many new roses look very similar to those we already grow. Most of them are lovely roses but so many disappear from catalogues in a few years. It takes a long time to displace an old favourite.

At the moment I am Chairman of the World Federation of Rose Societies Heritage Rose Committee – a job with many challenges but which has given me a great deal of pleasure, dealing with old friends and making new ones.

The first Heritage Rose group was the brainchild of Miriam Wilkins of El Cerrito, California, and was formed in 1975. Six regional branches were formed in the United States and together they made up the Heritage Rose Foundation.

Similar groups were subsequently established in Australia and New Zealand.

Hawera 1984

A small group of Australian, New Zealand and American heritage rose enthusiasts got together with the aim of setting up a world-wide organisation. This led to our first international conference in 1984, convened in New Zealand by Roger Springett, at Hawera near New Plymouth, with an attendance of 150 people from many different countries. I remember a brilliant lecture by Peg Smith of New Zealand, giving intriguing recipes for rose hip syrup, and for rose liqueur, using a litre of brandy – although one of the audience members reacted to the latter with 'What a waste!' Mary Cullinan, another fascinating speaker, traced the spread of the China roses brought out as cuttings by the early settlers.

Adelaide 1986

The next conference was in Adelaide in 1986, with Barbara Cannon talking about old roses in Spanish Mission gardens and their use in California. Gwen Fagan from South Africa spoke on historic roses that arrived at the Cape from both Europe and the Far East. Susan Irvine gave an excellent lecture on Alister Clark roses that included some lovely slides of the garden at Bulla in its heyday. Peter Beales showed some marvellous slides of huge old roses in England, growing up into trees and cascading downwards. 'Rambling Rector' and 'Sir Cedric Morris' were particularly magnificent. A plant of 'American Pillar' growing to the top of an electricity pole was a sight to remember – I wonder what the reaction would be from our Electricity Trust! After many other informative speakers the final lecture was given by Walter Duncan who spoke about bourbon roses. He was just the right person to conclude the lectures on a happy informal note.

Before the convention started, several busloads of visitors came to my garden in Renmark and I made a plea for some of the people on the final bus to stay behind and help pick roses for decorating the conference venue, The Colonial Function & Conference Centre at Glen Osmond. In the cool of the evening twelve of us, mainly New Zealanders, sallied forth and picked twenty buckets of old roses in an hour – and what a time we had.

Good friend Eric Trimper had come up from Adelaide to help and he and I set out at five o'clock next morning in a large van filled with forty buckets of roses and mixed flowers for the decorations. Several helpers ensured that the lovely old building was quickly transformed into a Victorian setting for the Heritage Conference.

I gave a tribute to the Old Masters, tracing the history of flower painting from Greek, Byzantine and early Roman times to the Renaissance, when the middle class became quite wealthy and loved to have the flowers they grew in their gardens painted. The early paintings were largely a collection of one of this and one of that. Done with great accuracy and detail, they are among the most beautiful flower paintings of all ages. For the flower arrangements to accompany this talk I managed to find the last tulips in the Dandenongs – a Flemish flower piece without tulips is not a Flemish flower piece. Most of the other flowers came from my garden. I would have loved to have located a fritillaria for the top of the arrangement, but I had to make do with an alstroemeria.

One of my arrangements at The Huntington. An alabaster urn holds soft blues and mauves, complementing the colour of the marble statue. Delphiniums and iris provide blue tonings, with roses, tulips, old-fashioned lilac, stocks and watsonias providing pink.

Los Angeles 1988

The famous mansion and garden The Huntington, at Los Angeles, California was the venue in 1988, with Evona Thompson lecturing on the paintings of Paul de Longpré, a Frenchman from Lyon who settled in the United States. He is now considered almost an American Redouté – praise indeed! Another highlight was Michele Courty-Schnapper on the evolution of the Roseraie du Val-du-Marne (better known to many as La Roseraie de l'Haÿ) south of Paris and now over a century old.

Before I gave my demonstration I was driven around The Huntington garden to pick flowers. I was allowed to choose blooms not only from the rose garden but also from the Shakespearean garden and the collection of exotic trees and shrubs. What an exciting range of plants! The Huntington garden is famous for its huge collection of camellias and garden-grown cacti and succulents. Its rose garden features a historic collection of old hybrid teas and floribundas, planted in long beds, one for each decade. Some of these are very rare.

An old copper bowl contains iris, lilies, *Rosa alba* 'Celeste' and *R. alba maxima* flowing downwards, both roses found in the early Flemish period. These combine with pink and white peonies, honeysuckle, artichokes, *Rosa foetida lutea*, *R. gallica* 'Tuscany' and anchusa for that touch of blue. Note the softening effect of the grey-green rose foliage, the fruit and the bird's nest with its blue-green eggs just visible.

Christchurch 1990

The fourth conference was in Christchurch in 1990 with a record attendance of 450. Here (as was to be the case in Cambridge in 1997 and Dunedin in 2005) we had university accommodation during the summer vacation at a very reasonable cost. A couple of elderly ladies remarked 'It's just like going back to boarding school. What fun!' while a couple of others took a taxi to five-star accommodation. I'm sure that we who stayed had a lot more fun.

A most amazing collection of flowers was at my disposal for use in the containers I had brought across the Tasman. My theme was 'Flower Arranging from 1600 to 1950'.

A simple ewer contains a lovely combination of cream foxgloves, stocks, aquilegias and 'Graham Thomas' roses as a tribute to that great gardener, author, painter and rosarian who re-introduced so many varieties of old roses that were in danger of being lost forever.

Adelaide 1993

For want of other applicants, Adelaide offered to host the next International Heritage Rose Conference in 1993.

A highlight was Bill Grant's slide show on Dr Gianfranco Fineschi's rose garden at Cavriglia, north of Rome, which was begun in 1961 and now houses one of the largest and most varied private collections in the world. The keynote speaker, Hazel le Rougetel from England, spoke on changing fashions in roses from the ninth to the twenty-first century – and they are still changing!

I gave a tribute to the rose, following the history of flower arranging from the early Renaissance until modern times, looking not only at roses but also other flowers and filler material, demonstrating while I spoke.

At Christchurch two alabaster containers on a marble-topped table hold a lovely combination of mauve-pink peonies, delphiniums, deutzias and opium poppies with their grey-green leaves. So dominant were the peonies that one of the audience quipped how she enjoyed the peony demonstration! Gallica roses 'Charles de Mills' and 'Tuscany' were coupled with the damasks 'Mme Hardy' and 'Chloris'. This arrangement was done in the Rococo style favoured in France at the time of Louis XV.

Los Angeles 1996

The Huntington was again the venue in 1996, with Roger Phillips, writer and television star, speaking about hunting for lost roses in China. Rosamund Wallinger described 'The Renaissance of a 1908 Jekyll Garden at Upton Grey' – her garden in England – which she has restored to its original Gertrude Jekyll plan.

Up to this point I had gently coerced (or should I say, bullied) my New Zealand, Australian and American friends into holding conferences. From now on it was much easier with other countries offering to host them.

In a silver épergne I used only roses with their own foliage to fill out the arrangement. Roses included 'Variegata di Bologna', 'Tuscany Superb', 'Duchesse de Montebello' and 'Jacques Cartier'. This arrangement was also made at Christchurch.

Cambridge 1997

The seventh conference was held in England, at the University of Cambridge, during the summer vacation in 1997.

Once again I demonstrated arrangements of the Old Masters. After a month of rain the roses were rather waterlogged but the peonies, campanulas and lilies, as well as the trees and shrubs, were looking good. I managed to get some nice mauve tulips and some beautiful sweet williams. I discovered, strangely enough, that tulips were very hard to obtain in Belgium where I was to go next, to demonstrate at Hex Castle. After the demonstration at Cambridge, the tulips I had

A garland of roses picked for me by Chairman Peter Beales in pouring rain. It is arranged around a Madonna and Child and sacrificial lamb by da Vinci. The roses include 'Mme Hardy', *Rosa gallica officinalis*, 'Rosa Mundi', 'Tuscany', *Rosa alba semi-plena* and 'Tricolore de Flandre', almost all authentic to the period.

used were stored in the refrigerator of the college in which we were billeted, to be taken to Belgium. By the time I got to Hex Castle they were wilting a bit, so I said they were a new variety called 'Tristesse', which means 'sad', much to the amusement of the delegates. (I had put some sweet williams in another refrigerator but they came out frozen solid and completely useless.)

A highlight for me was taking a tour of the Cambridge conference delegates to the university's Fitzwilliam Museum, with its two large rooms filled with paintings of the Old Flemish, Dutch and French Masters.

Visits to Hay Hill, headquarters of the Royal National Rose Society, to Hatfield House, home of the Marchioness of Salisbury, with its sunken Elizabethan garden containing only plants used at that time, and the two beautiful private gardens and nurseries of Peter Beales and David Austin, were all very special.

Lyon 1999

The most magical conference of all was at Lyon in 1999, organised by the dynamic and extremely knowledgeable Odile Masquelier. Lectures were memorable, with Professor Gianfranco Fineschi talking on 'Pernetiana Roses of the First Thirty Years of the Twentieth Century' – the most brilliant lecture I have ever heard! It received a unanimous standing ovation. The Pernetiana roses brought brilliant yellows, copper-gold, oranges and salmon colourings into modern roses – a terrific advance.

We attended an evening soiree in Odile and Georges Masquelier's garden on a hilltop overlooking the confluence of the Rhone and Saone Rivers. The floodlit garden with hundreds of old roses and climbers on pergolas, all at their peak, was sheer magic, as was the food and drink.

The final gala dinner, at Chez Bocuse on the banks of the Rhone at l'Abbaye de Colognes, was a glittering affair, with all the food held high in the air by the waiters coming down a steep curved staircase to the sound of music. The famous chef, Paul Bocuse, for whom Guillot named a rose, will be remembered forever by the 290 delegates who were present.

Charleston 2001

The ninth conference was held at Charleston in the United States, in October 2001. Emphasis was on the noisette roses which originated there. I could not attend this as we were told not to travel so soon after the September 11 bombing.

I used flowers from the Middleton Place garden – delphiniums, iris, daisies, salvias, tulips, perennial phlox, 'Cecile Brunner' roses and red amaranthus – to match the dwarf red globe artichokes I had not seen before.

However, I was asked to speak and demonstrate at the 150th anniversary of the Charleston Horticultural Society in 2005, held at Middleton Place, an old pre-Civil War mansion, a relic of the rice plantations with magnificent old trees and superb camellias.

Because of my busy schedule, I left viewing the garden until my final day in Charleston, which was a mistake as it poured with rain and everything was awash, bringing home to me why rice was grown there so successfully! My hostess was Ruth Knopf, one of the world's experts on teas, noisettes and China roses. I was most impressed with the use of noisette roses in the gardens of the lovely old homes in the centre of the city, which was still unspoilt by modern development. There were also great noisette collections at Hampton Park and Boone Hall.

Sangerhausen 2003

The 2003 conference at the great German Rosarium in Sangerhausen was organised by the WFRS for the centenary celebrations. It was very successful. Unfortunately I could not attend because of a health problem.

Dunedin 2005

Dunedin hosted the tenth conference in 2005, with 350 delegates attending. It was very well planned with a choice of lectures on many subjects. Odile Masquelier spoke on 'The Nineteenth Century Wizards of Lyon', the rose breeders who brought new colours into our modern roses.

I made seven arrangements, basing them on the Old Masters who painted from the early seventeenth century, such as Jan Brueghel (1568–1625) and Ambrosius Bosschaert (1573–1621), eighteenth century painters such as Jan Van Huysum (1682–1749) and Jan van Os (1774–1808), up until Victorian times when the épergne became a popular arrangement medium for the dining room table.

A banquet was held in the lovely old town hall, built in the gold-rush days. With Dunedin taking great pride in its Scottish heritage, the sound of bagpipes filled the air … and there was haggis.

We were enthralled with our visit to the old Northern Cemetery maintained by Heritage Rose Society members; there are 1000 old Victorian roses cascading over obelisks and graves – a magic and serene place which is a must on a visit to New Zealand. The private gardens we visited were all stunning, with magnificent roses and a vast array of matching bulbs and perennials.

Chaalis 2007

The next great conference was again in France in 2007 and organised by Professor Francois Joyaux in the medieval Royal Abbey of Chaalis at Fontaine-Chaalis, north of Paris. There was an imposing ruin of a Cistercian monastery and a delightful walled rose garden created by André Gamard in 1998. Roses were at their peak and a pergola of pale pink 'New Dawn' looked just right with a background of ancient stone walling.

The speakers were very well chosen – Odile Masquelier, Helga Brichet, Peter Boyd from England on Scots roses and Dr Yuki Mikanagi from Japan on rose pigments – were all fascinating to listen to, as was Viru Viraraghavan on breeding evergreen roses for warm climates using *Rosa gigantea* and *R. clinophylla*, species that will grow in the delta of the Ganges where it can be almost submerged for months.

There were visits to Rheims Cathedral, Bagatelle, Roseraie de l'Haÿ, Malmaison, the Royal Academy and to Professor Joyaux's collection of gallicas.

Sakura 2011

There was to have been a conference in Madeira in 2009, but this had to be postponed. However, in 2011 Sakura, a city just north of Tokyo, is planning a marvellous conference specialising in roses of the Orient where so many of our roses for breeding new strains have originated. This will be a very special event.

HERITAGE ROSES IN AUSTRALIA

The early part of the twentieth century saw the advent of modern hybrid teas and later, in the 1940s, floribundas. These roses had four or five flushes per year and so slowly replaced the old once-blooming roses. We must realise that in hotter areas of Australia old roses have a much shorter flowering period than they do in southern Victoria, Tasmania and the South Island of New Zealand. They also have much smaller blooms.

Tea roses, however, began regaining popularity in these hotter areas because of their ability to survive in drought conditions without shedding their foliage. When the autumn rains begin they burst into wonderful new growth. China roses are also great survivors, developing into very large bushes with twiggy growth and massive crops of flowers. Noisettes such as 'Bouquet d'Or', 'Crépuscule', 'Lamarque' and 'Mme Berard' produce good autumn flushes and remain evergreen. This makes them ideal for covering old sheds and fences.

There was a revival of interest in old roses from those buying old houses where they wanted plants from that period. This applied particularly to National Trust properties.

Castlemaine 1991

The revival of interest in old roses led to the first national conference of Heritage Roses in Australia, which was organised by the Victorian Goldfields group in the historic town of Castlemaine in central Victoria during November 1991. One hundred and twenty delegates attended from all Australian states with eight folk from New Zealand.

The conference began with an illustrated lecture on 'Orientation to Goldfields Gardens' by Sarah Guest, well-known Victorian writer and journalist. Sarah's description of some of the lovely gardens in the area whetted our appetites for what we were to see during the garden tours. Particularly appealing were the cottage gardens around the old miners' cottages – most picturesque but very difficult to maintain.

Clive Winmill, a local identity, talked about his 'Twenty Years with Roses'. I was lucky enough to visit his garden of unpruned plants cascading down a hillside while they were at their peak. I agreed with Clive when he said, 'Never give a name to an unknown rose unless you are certain you are correct and have grown and observed the variety at close hand.'

I gave a demonstration with old roses, David Austin roses and cottage-type plants arranged in antique containers. The roses had kept well considering they had travelled all the way from Renmark and were the last remnants of the spring flush.

Tommy Garnett, the great old gardener and writer who developed the garden of St Erth, at Blackwood in Victoria, dealt with the life of Alister Clark and his garden at Glenara. Tommy's talk really brought the Clark family and its roses, daffodils and racehorses to life. Susan Irvine spoke about Australian-bred roses and the great work of many of our local breeders.

The final lecture, 'Garden Design with Roses', was presented by English author and gardener, Suzanne Price. She showed many ways of using roses in garden design, with special emphasis on climbers on pergolas, arches, walls and structures – I feel that we don't use climbers as much as we should, but then we don't have those lovely mellow brick walls every garden in England seems to have!

What impressed everyone at this conference was the friendly atmosphere, the wonderful food put on every couple of hours by various organisations and, above all, the terrific effort of the convenors.

At a meeting of coordinators from all regions of Australia, it was decided to elect a Committee of Management from South Australia to host the next conference. I was chosen as President.

Adelaide 1993

South Australia hosted the second conference in 1993, which was also an International Conference and written about earlier in this chapter. I retired from my position as President, handing over to the new co-presidents Gillian Batchen and Peter Cox from New South Wales.

Orange 1995

In 1995 Heritage Roses held its third conference in Orange, New South Wales, in the high country west of Sydney. We saw some huge gardens filled with roses, azaleas and rhododendrons, as well as the famous Orange Botanical Gardens with its new area of rose species looked after by the local Heritage Rose group.

The theme of the conference was 'Species Roses'. In the first lecture, Colonel Kevin Hughes discussed in great depth the classification of the genus *Rosa* with its 150 species. This was accompanied by excellent slides.

Bill Grant from California described how his species roses grow in semi-shade under coastal oak trees, some climbing up the trees before cascading downwards. Many of them have fine autumn foliage and spectacular hips which last for months.

Next was that incomparable pair, Roger Phillips and Martyn Rix from England. Their topic was their rose quest in China and the excitement of finding *Rosa gigantea* and *R. longicuspis* in the wild, as well as the many China roses growing in gardens that are not available elsewhere. Fortunately, the soft pink 'Lijiang Road Climber' which they found is now available in Australia. Bred from *Rosa gigantea*, it covers itself in early spring with masses of semi-double flowers that show up well against the glossy foliage.

Other lectures were given by Trisha Dixon on 'Roses in Country Gardens', and by Milton Simms on 'The Synstylae Ramblers' which are so suitable for large country gardens.

Fremantle 1997

The historic port of Fremantle was chosen by Western Australia as the place to host the fourth Heritage Rose Conference in 1997. The theme was 'Heritage Roses in our Ancient Land'.

The conference began with a bus trip south of Perth, viewing many amazing gardens at Pinjarra, Kojonup, Mt Barker and Albany. All were in excellent condition, filled with old roses cascading in all directions and planted among collections of old bulbs and perennials. Overseas visitors were astonished to see watsonias and arum lilies growing wild along the roads – escapees from gardens!

I could not participate in the tour, unfortunately, as I had brought with me six boxes of cut roses and other flowers for a demonstration. The boxes were singled out by a sniffer dog at Perth Airport, much to my surprise, as I'd been told there were no restrictions on getting flowers into Western Australia. After twenty-four hours and many phone calls between Departments of Agriculture it was all resolved. Fortunately, the boxes had been put into a cool room and the flowers were still useable. This is always a worry when travelling.

In my demonstration I traced the changing styles in flower arranging over the years. Other speakers included John Viska and Milton Simms, Sean McCann from Ireland and Sally Allison from New Zealand. Walter Duncan, Maureen Ross and I made up a panel for a symposium on 'Our Ten Best Roses'. There was much repartee and many questions from the floor with an amazing number of roses discussed and discarded before the final ten were chosen.

To close the conference, we visited nine beautiful and highly original gardens in the city area followed by a tour of seven large gardens in the Perth Hills. The climate there is wetter and cooler, allowing the garden owners to grow beautiful cool climate perennials.

Geelong 1999

I could not attend the fifth conference which was held in Geelong in 1999, but I believe it was outstanding.

Of course there was a visit to the Geelong Botanical Gardens with its comprehensive collection of salvias that stand up so well to drought. A bus trip to the Western Districts, famous for their fine wool merino sheep studs, stately early Victorian mansions and huge gardens, was well patronised and enjoyed by all.

Lectures included Bill Grant from California on 'Rugosa Roses', so good in sandy soils and coastal conditions. Gwen Fagan, author of *Roses at the Cape of Good Hope*, spoke about some of the world's significant rose gardens and the way one can landscape with roses. The great rose breeder from Kordes Roses, Wilhelm Kordes, grandson of founder, Wilhelm Kordes I, discussed the roses they had bred, starting with 'Crimson Glory' in 1936.

Hahndorf 2001

When South Australia hosted the sixth biennial conference in 2001 in the Adelaide Hills township of Hahndorf, the topic was 'Reaching for the Sky', with the emphasis on climbing roses.

I did a demonstration as part of the opening, on the topic 'From Federation to the New Millennium', using teas, noisettes and old hybrid teas such as 'La France' and 'Mme Abel Chatenay' in period containers. I moved on to the Edwardian era when ramblers were in vogue, the art nouveau period and Constance Spry's genius, to bowls and troughs, then urns and finally pedestals and modern arranging using a minimum of flowers to great effect.

Keynote speaker, Steve Scanniello from New York, spoke twice. From the United States came the *Rosa setigera* hybrids, using crosses with noisette roses to produce vigorous climbers such as 'Long John Silver' and 'Baltimore Belle'. *Rosa wichurana* was used to produce a multitude of ramblers such as 'Dorothy Perkins', 'Dr W. Van Fleet' and 'American Pillar'. All of these flowered only once until a chance cutting of 'Dr W. Van Fleet' produced repeat flowers and was named 'New Dawn'. This plant was used in the breeding of most of the repeat-flowering climbers we grow today, such as 'Handel', 'Bantry Bay' and 'Dublin Bay'.

In the second talk, the Barbier group of ramblers, such as 'Albertine', 'Alexandre Girault' and 'François Juranville', were discussed. These are seen at their best in such gardens as La Roseraie de l'Haÿ in Paris and Odile Masquelier's magic garden at La Bonne Maison in Lyon.

Sally Allison from Christchurch spoke about climbers and ramblers for small gardens using, as one example, thornless roses such as 'Donna Maria', 'Zéphirine Drouhin' and her paler sports 'Kathleen Harrop' and 'Martha', as well as the boursault 'Amadis' with its glorious autumn foliage.

Viru Viraraghavan, the well-known species expert from India, spoke of the species roses grown in India and his use of *Rosa gigantea* and *R. clinophylla*. He aims to produce evergreen roses that will cope with hot summers as well as new tea roses, so popular in warm climates.

There were excellent workshops. Sally Allison described suitable structures for roses including her famous 'rosebo', a very large rose-covered gazebo, which seats sixty people beneath it.

Tina Miljanovic, curator of the species rose collection at Mt Lofty Botanic Gardens, followed with the identification of climbing roses.

Girija Viraraghavan's workshop described rose products, their history and use in many areas – medicinal, cosmetic and dietary. Her descriptions of rose oils, syrups, sherbets, rosewater and rose petal jams were fascinating.

Walter Duncan gave advice on training climbers to increase flowering. His use of a blackboard to illustrate tying up and pegging down was very entertaining.

Maureen Ross dealt brilliantly with climbing teas, early hybrid teas and polyanthas from 1900 to 1950, many of which are still popular today.

Garden visits included the collection of old roses at Urrbrae House, the North Bank Heritage Rose Garden on the River Torrens and The Cedars at Hahndorf, home of Sir Hans Heysen, where the roses he painted are still growing. Other trips included gardens in the Adelaide Hills and several in the Barossa Valley. The tour ended in my garden which luckily was at its flowering peak.

Hay 2003

The seventh National Heritage Rose Conference was held in 2003 in central New South Wales, at the Riverina township of Hay, situated on the Murrumbidgee River and famous for its merino sheep. The proceedings were brilliantly organised by a small group of volunteers under the capable supervision of Coleen and David Houston.

I started off the lectures with a demonstration on 'Roses in the Outback', using old roses in rustic pots as well as in antique containers from the homes of early squatters – teapots, wine coolers, gravy boats and alabaster urns – that had been handed down over the years.

Coleen Houston described coping with 'droughts and flooding rains', dust storms and locust plagues, as well as providing shelter for tender plants in a garden on the treeless plains around Hay.

Popular American gardening author, Bill Grant, talked of the old warrior roses of the past, from 'Adam' in 1838, the great parent of many modern roses, to 'Lady Mary Fitzwilliam' in 1882, 'Mme Caroline Testout' in 1901, 'Frau Karl Druschki' in 1901, still the whitest of all roses, red 'Etoile de Hollande' in 1919, the incomparable single 'Dainty Bess' in 1925, through to the autumn-coloured 'Talisman' – a new breakthrough in colour – in 1929.

Trish Dixon, a brilliant professional, gave hints to amateur photographers. Jane Zammit and Barbara May enthralled the audience with their lecture on identifying the roses in the huge old Rookwood Cemetery in Sydney, opened in 1867, where about a hundred old rose varieties have been found.

This was followed by well-known Churchill scholar, Pat Toolan, who described the roses she found in her travels through cemeteries in Australia, New Zealand, the United States and Europe. There was much interest in the "Buffalo Rose", brought out by settlers in the first ship to South Australia in 1836.

Nurseryman John Nieuwesteeg, from Victoria, talked of the roses bred by early Australians, and Richard Walsh ended the lecture programme with a look at the future with special reference to his own breeding programme. This was a perfect ending to a unique conference.

The trip we then took to outback gardens was a very special experience for us all.

Margaret River 2006

The picturesque Margaret River Region in Western Australia's south-west hosted the eighth Conference in 2006, using the theme 'Smell the Roses – Taste the Wine', as Margaret River is a premium wine-growing area.

Garden tours revealed what can be achieved in gardens with good winter rainfall but drought conditions in summer. Companion plantings of Mediterranean and Australian species were brilliantly done, and the use of various mulches and ground covers was widespread. The climbing roses, sprawling over anything from old clothes hoists to gigantic trees, arbours of long-lasting hardwoods and bales of hay three or four high nicked from the feedshed, were as spectacular as they were varied.

Knowledgeable plantsman Gregg Lowery, from California, started the programme with the noisettes and hybrid musks which had been admired in so many of the local gardens. Gregg considers that noisettes such as 'Rêve d'Or', 'Crépuscule', Duchesse d'Auerstadt', 'Lamarque' and 'William Allen Richardson' have more flushes in a year than any other climbing rose.

Laurie Newman from Victoria spoke of his involvement in donating and planting a collection of species roses in the Beijing Botanical Garden in China. A group of Australians visited this garden in April 2010 and were delighted to see that the plants were all flourishing.

I gave a brief talk on the World Federation of Rose Societies and

'Rêve d'Or'.
(*Photograph courtesy Julie Lack*)

its aim of making a list of all the major historic rose collections in the world – of which there are many.

Phillip Robinson, who with partner Gregg Lowery has one of the largest collections of all classes of roses in the world at Vintage Gardens in Sebastopol, California, dealt with early hybrid teas up to 1945. Many of these are in danger of becoming extinct. It was interesting to learn that some of the most popular varieties had produced many sports of different colours.

Bob Melville discussed rootstocks, especially *Rosa* x *fortuneana*, so important in the sandy coastal plains of Western Australia.

Frenchman Jocelen Janon, now residing in New Zealand, spoke with great charm of his love affair with the tea roses bred by Nabonnand in France from 1887 to 1924. It is amazing how many roses bred during this period are named after titled ladies – not many after men!

The doyenne of old rose lovers, Odile Masquelier of La Bonne Maison, enthralled her audience with a slide tour of her garden, starting with 'Maréchal Niel' in her greenhouse in very early spring and ending with hips and frost on 'Nozomi', with the garden covered in snow. A trip through a year with roses and an unforgettable experience for us all made a fitting climax to the lecture programme.

The post-convention tour ended in the amazing garden of Patricia Routley at Northcliffe in the south-west corner of Western Australia, snuggled into the edge of a great karri forest and containing a huge collection of found roses. Gregg Lowery, Phillip Robinson and I had great fun suggesting possible names to Patricia amid much arguing and amusing repartee.

Mornington 2008

In November 2008 Victoria hosted the ninth Australian Heritage Rose Conference, entitled 'Keeping History Alive'. This was held in the beautiful late Victorian mansion Morning Star, at Mornington, a lovely seaside town south-east of Melbourne. Judy Barrett, the owner of Morning Star, has planted a rose garden of magnificent proportions with 30 000 bushes, many of them laden with blooms when I was there.

The Victorian ballroom was used for the main conference

proceedings. I had beautified it with flowers placed in four huge fibreglass urns. The urns had been used for a wedding the week before and Judy had managed to retain them for the conference. Additionally, I made eight other large arrangements for various rooms that were to be used during the conference. I then demonstrated for the opening evening with the theme 'Arranging Roses through Australia's History'. It was a very happy but exhausting day.

A large fibreglass urn holds huge stems of multi-headed 'Queen Elizabeth' roses mixed with blue delphiniums and iris, acanthus, Queen Anne's lace and blue gum leaves. I didn't want to hide those most amazing handles.

At the back of the room similar flowers were used. Notice the airy use of Queen Anne's lace and blue gum foliage.

On the other side of the stage was a similar arrangement, this time using deep pink assorted roses – 'Peter Frankenfeld', 'Pink Silk' and 'Baronne E. de Rothschild' with a more mauve tinge. The array of acanthus flowers, used to give height, ties in with the colour of the urns.

One of a pair of black cast-iron urns decorating the conference room, containing cotinus and the roses 'Abraham Darby', 'Charles Austin', 'Yellow Charles Austin' and 'Graham Thomas', with a few yellow kniphofias for height.

This is a lavish Flemish concoction using flowers and fruit. White crinums, delphiniums and aquilegias are at the top with red and white peonies, iris, sunflowers, *Rosa gallica officinalis* and tulips cascading downwards, with 'Rose de Rescht' for added vibrancy. Brown iris and a bent-stemmed opium poppy with its lovely foliage add interest at the right. The bird's nest, artichokes, ornamental corn, lemons and cut blood oranges bring the eye down to the front. The terracotta urn ties in well.

My cast-iron container is filled with bronze *Cotinus* 'Royal Purple' to tie in with the colour of the figurine. The highlight is a mass of striped 'Camille Pisarro', one of Delbard's best roses. These are combined with apricot spuria iris and a few kniphofias.

Here a cast-iron gentleman container holds a mass of 'Gold Medal' roses, tulips, blue salvia and blue iris.

A collection of my arrangements for the conference. Notice the surtout of rambling roses and silver bowl of mixed teas.

Brisbane 2010

The tenth conference was in Brisbane in October 2010, on the topic was 'The Subtropics: Rainforest to Roses'. In Brisbane tea roses grow very well, forming huge bushes. They are also planted in gardens west of the Great Dividing Range, on the Darling Downs, where they stand up to droughts, flooding rains and locust plagues! Because the Renmark Rose Festival and the unveiling of the David Ruston sculpture coincided with this conference I was unable to attend, but I understand that there were great gardens, magnificent food and very friendly hospitality.

Mount Gambier 2012

The next conference will be in 2012 at Mount Gambier, in South Australia's green south-east. The venue is to be a huge old barn surrounded by rambling cottage gardens and superb exotic trees, a perfect setting for old roses.

Chapter 6

Remembered Gardens

Sangerhausen 1983
(Condensed from an article published in *The Australian Rose Annual* 1984, page 139.)

For many years Heather Rumsey had corresponded with Herr Ingomar Lang, Director of the Sangerhausen Rosarium in East Germany, and both she and I had long wished to visit. So in 1983, complete with applications for visas and a permit to spend three days at the Rosarium prior to the World Rose Convention at Baden-Baden, we took a train from Frankfurt.

When we entered the gates we were enthralled. The great Sangerhausen Rosarium (now the Europa-Rosarium) was planted early in 1900 by Professor Ewald Gnau and contains an overwhelming collection of old roses as well as thousands of hybrid teas and floribundas. It consists of four sections, all beautifully landscaped, with a background of cold climate trees which give an excellent backdrop and a woodland effect to the whole setting, so different

An overview of Sangerhausen showing the woodland effect of the garden. The 150 m 'pyramid' in the background is a mine dump called Hohe Linde that contains about 20 million tons of deadrock.

Wichurana ramblers trained up larch poles at Sangerhausen Rosarium.

from the formal symmetry of many French and German rose gardens. The oldest section at the entrance is more formal than the remainder, with many of the beds of regular shapes surrounded by clipped box edging. However, the pride of this area is the multiflora and wichurana ramblers trained on larch poles against a background of trees. The effect of different heights, with some of the roses reaching seven metres, was a sight I will never forget.

The next part of the garden was almost a woodland setting, with open areas towards the centre, where beds of hybrid teas and floribundas were set informally in lawns. These roses were all pruned to ground level after damage from the cold in winter and were planted very close together, almost as in a nursery bed. I was impressed with the planting of similar shades together, the pale pinks and creams, in particular, looking delightful. I must mention the tea roses, growing in such a cold climate, so far removed from where we would expect them to grow. Their section was the warmest part of the garden and each winter the plants were completely covered with soil and fir branches for protection. The highlight of this part of the garden was the huge beds of almost unpruned albas, gallicas, mosses, damasks, centifolias and bourbons set in the lawns at random in a delightfully natural way. The huge bushes unaffected by the cold (no China blood here) cascaded over the edges of the beds with an incredible display of hundreds of flowers per bush.

The third part of the garden contained some modern sculpture which I did not think helped the old roses at all, while the fourth part of the garden was formal in design and planted with all the classes, well grouped, with straight cement paths connecting the beds. Here the hybrid musks were stupendous, with great arching bushes laden with flowers and scent – 'Felicia', 'Penelope', 'Prosperity', 'Pink Prosperity', 'Aurora', 'Cornelia', 'Moonlight', 'Buff Beauty' and 'Autumn Delight' were some of the best specimens that I have seen growing anywhere, the bushes clothed in flowers to ground level. At the far end of the garden was a well-landscaped artificial hill, with a glorious view down the centre of the garden, containing a very simple memorial to Professor Gnau.

It was not only the roses that enthralled me at Sangerhausen, it was all those cold-climate perennials that we find difficult to grow. Huge great peonies with dozens of flowers on each bush, yellow *Eremurus* (foxtail lilies) in a large bed, a deep violet erigeron, masses of *Veronica incana*, a lovely display of *Salvia superba* and huge delphiniums, shasta daisies, perennial phlox and liliums, with a pond nearby with a tremendous plant of gunnera.

I will never forget Sangerhausen, the greatest collection of roses in the world, in a superb natural setting in a harsh climate, with the pillars, 200 varieties in all, showing up so well against the background of lovely old trees. It was a garden in which old roses could grow unchecked and show themselves as the most graceful of flowering shrubs, without the hard pruning and regimentation of such great gardens as La Roseraie de l'Haÿ in Paris. The pilgrimage to Sangerhausen was a great success. Thank you, Herr Lang, the Director, for having us. It was an experience I will remember forever.

A Tour of Rose Gardens in Europe and England 1988

(Condensed from an article published in *The Australian Rose Annual* 1989, page 75.)

On 20 June 1988, sixteen folk set off from Adelaide to Zurich, on a tour organised by Elders IXL and led by me.

Our first visit was to the beautiful old medieval village of Rapperswil to visit Lotte and Willi Günthart. I had met the Güntharts at several World Federation conferences where Lotte's superb rose paintings had been exhibited, and it was marvellous to see her old studio housed in the ancient Rote Rose Inn. Her paintings of 'Fantin Latour', 'Empress Josephine' and 'Golden Wings' were brilliant. The back of the studio sloped steeply down into a lovely Swiss valley and was planted with roses old and new. A pergola was smothered with 'New Dawn' at its peak and great bushes of 'Mme Isaac Pereire' and the creamy white 'City of York' clothed the walls of the inn. A bed of the McGredy 'hand-painted' rose, 'Regensberg', created a lot of interest, just the right variety to be named after such a beautiful village. Lotte had planted a long bed of the 'Lotte Günthart' rose, a huge crimson flower with a quartered centre which looked like a peony, together with 'Peace', which she had painted when it became the winner of the first World's Favourite Rose competition. The third variety planted was 'Princess de Monaco' in memory of a great friend. Unfortunately, 'Princess de Monaco' turned out to be 'Princess Margaret' – a right royal mix-up.

The Güntharts lived in a lovely old house across the street from the inn with a garden filled with peonies, delphiniums, clematis and roses, with the dusky red 'Guinée' climbing up the house walls.

We then walked through the village to Lotte's third garden, which cascaded down the valley – all roses unpruned and allowed to develop to their full potential. 'Complicata', 'Variegata di Bologna', 'Charles de Mills', 'Cardinal Richelieu', 'Ulrich Brunner Fils' and 'Empress Josephine' had to be seen to be believed – bushes 2.5 metres high and as much across, laden with flowers of superb quality and right at their peak.

We stayed for a couple of days at Lindau, an ancient town on an island in Lake Constance. The entrance to Lindau was unique with hundreds of Kordes shrub roses trained along the ancient stone walls – a sight to be remembered forever.

We then caught a boat to the great garden of Mainau and were delighted with what we saw. Some of the garden has to be covered with glass for winter protection. The old roses here were amazing – gigantic bushes of 'Clair Matin', 'Smarty', 'Mme Plantier', 'Mme Hardy', 'Urdh' and 'Venusta Pendula' were planted each side of a long curved path and filled the air with perfume. Magnificent trees 200 years old abounded, with limes, tulip trees and ginkgos, and the *Cotinus* 'Royal Purple' was outstanding. The children's garden contained mammoth ducks, a peacock and an owl, all made of plants within a hidden frame. The Italianate garden at the side of the Schloss was beautiful, with standard and weeping roses to give height and hard-pruned bedding roses beneath. Two gigantic pillars of 'Till Uhlenspiegel' dominated the garden and pergolas were covered with climbers and ramblers.

We travelled through Switzerland to Geneva to visit Le Parc de la Grange on the shores of the lake. This small rose garden was really lovely and here again weeping standards were the highlights – 'Paul's Scarlet Climber', 'Albertine', 'American Pillar' and 'New Dawn' used as weepers. The hybrid tea rose 'Château de Versailles' was the most outstanding hybrid tea I saw anywhere, brilliant red with a silver reverse, wonderful form and amazing petal texture on a good bush with first-class foliage. It came on the market in Australia as 'Guy Laroche' and was bred by Delbard.

From Geneva we crossed into France to visit Lyon, home of most of the great rose breeders of the nineteenth century, and see La Roseraie Internationale du Parc de la Tête d'Or. This garden, although a little past its spring peak, was magnificent. Unlike most European public gardens it was more natural, with curved rose beds set in lawn among trees and lakes. It was Saturday afternoon and we counted sixteen wedding parties in full regalia, mostly Italian, being photographed in succession in all the best spots. We were amused to see the 'best men' carrying huge baskets of flowers and holding them up for each fresh photograph. How the guests managed to find the right wedding I do not know!

Our next port of call was Le Parc Floral de la Source at Orléans south of Paris – probably the loveliest rose garden we saw in Europe. The garden also contained a marvellous iris collection which unfortunately had completely finished flowering. Bearded iris flower in Europe six weeks before the roses, whereas in Australia they usually peak just a few days beforehand. Also, old roses flower several weeks before hybrid teas and floribundas in Europe and it is the reverse in Australia. I put this down to the China 'blood' in our modern roses, which means they never go completely dormant in our warm winters, and then shoot much earlier in comparison to other plants than they do in Europe. There were excellent plantings of perennials, herbs and a lovely background of trees at Orléans and a beautiful rose garden set in grass beside an expanse of water called Le Miroir, which provided a fitting setting for an old chateau on a hill on the opposite side of the lake. Roses that impressed me were in a section devoted to roses raised by Georges Delbard – 'Mme V. Dimitriu' and 'Grand Siècle' – complemented by cyclamen all in shades of pink. A cream climber called 'Croix Blanche' was outstanding with flowers of great substance.

The next garden we visited was Le Jardin de Bagatelle in the Bois de Boulogne, in the heart of Paris. This was a formal rose garden with raked gravel paths, clipped box edging to all beds and roses set in grass, often with a standard of the same variety in each bed to give height. Again, weeping standards were very well used, with 'American Pillar', 'New Dawn', 'Heidelberg', 'Dorothy Perkins', 'Swany', 'François Juranville' and 'Excelsa' outstanding. Of the bedded roses,

The formal rose garden at Parc de Bagatelle.

'Centenaire de Lourdes' bred by Delbard-Chabert in 1958 stole the show. This rose is soft rose pink in colour, semi-double with fifteen to twenty wavy petals on a very rounded bush like 'Iceberg'. The flowers keep their colour well and this variety is excellent as a standard.

Four of us took the opportunity to visit Monet's garden at Giverny, downstream from Paris, on a free day. Here roses were combined very well with poppies, nasturtiums, cornflowers, peonies, nicotania and geraniums, in fact all the flowers that Monet painted so brilliantly. Straight paths were softened by the exuberant planting tumbling over them. Pergolas and arches were festooned with 'New Dawn', 'Excelsa', 'Dorothy Perkins' and 'American Pillar', and groups of 'Comte de Chambord' and old gallicas were used among the perennial plants to good effect. In complete contrast to the formal garden was the water-lily area across the road, which included a large lake completely surrounded and enclosed by a most beautifully grouped collection of shrubs and trees.

In between viewing the splendour of the Louvre, Versailles and Vaux le Vicomte, we visited the great rose garden of La Roseraie de l'Haÿ in an outer suburb of Paris. This garden contains one of the finest collection of old roses in the world, with climbing roses outstanding. There are sections for species, teas, gallicas, albas, bourbons et cetera, and a huge collection of polyantha varieties. Most of the old roses were past their prime but among the polyanthas 'Souvenir d'Adolphe Turc', 'Chatillon Rose', 'Rodhatte' and 'Gabrielle Privat' were still in good shape and so were the climbers 'Thalia' and the beautiful pale

Archways of wichurana ramblers at Roseraie de l'Haÿ.

Displays of climbing roses at Roseraie de l'Haÿ with the white multiflora rambler 'Thalia' in the foreground.

apricot pink 'Breeze Hill', while 'Long John Silver', with its quartered flowers in clusters of pearly white, was the loveliest – an interesting rose bred from the prairie rose, *Rosa setigera.*

From Paris we drove through glorious country to Brussels, diverting down country lanes in Belgium to visit the garden of a former World President of the World Federation of Rose Societies, Baronne Lily de Gerlache de Gomery, where we were given a delightful lunch. The garden was approaching its peak with hard-pruned bushes producing excellent quality flowers. It was strange to look down at the deep red blooms of 'Charles Mallerin' at knee height, rather than having to use a step-ladder as at home. It was interesting to see a long border of the old polyantha roses 'Rodhatte' and 'Joseph Guy' grown as a feature along the central axis of the garden.

From Brussels we crossed the Channel by hovercraft to England to visit Great Dixter, home of garden writer Christopher Lloyd, en route to Sissinghurst Castle on Wimbledon finals day. It poured with rain for the duration of our stay. It was my fifth visit to Sissinghurst and it looked the best I had ever seen it. The white garden looked superb from the Elizabethan Tower and 'Gloire de Dijon' lit up an old stone wall. The old roses were at their peak, underplanted with most interesting perennials such as *Malva moschata alba*, blue *Campanula lactiflora*, silvery *Eryngium giganteum* (Miss Willmott's Ghost), silver *Artemisia splendens* and huge heads of onion-like *Allium christophii*. A specimen of the New Zealand shrub *Hoheria lyallii* was gorgeous, and outstanding among the old roses were 'Rosa Mundi', 'Gloire de France', 'Charles de Mills', 'Camaieux', 'Portlandica' and 'Constance Spry'. Photography was impossible and I had to purchase a huge red National Trust umbrella for protection from the deluge. This later came in handy as a means of identification from afar!

Near Brighton we visited the Nymans Garden, which had been devastated by the gales of October 1987 when eighty per cent of the trees were uprooted, including twenty of the twenty-eight species which had been classified as the largest specimens of their kind in the British Isles. The town of Seven Oaks, famous for its seven aged oaks, suddenly became just Two Oaks! The devastation in the woods was still very evident. Kew and Wakehurst Place had suffered badly also, but for most of us who did not know the gardens beforehand, they still looked good.

It was then on to Wisley Gardens where the roses looked in good condition and then to Queen Mary's Rose Garden in Regents Park, where the great festoons of rambling roses – *Rosa longicuspis*, 'Bobbie James' and 'Wedding Day' – on the rope and pillar circular arbour had to be seen to be believed. The bedding roses made good displays, best of all being a large bed of 'Savoy Hotel', a pretty pink exhibition rose of great form and size.

We then travelled to St Albans and the excitement of the Great Summer Show, and what a spectacle it was. The Spanish Armada was the theme and the design by Krees van Deel was outstanding. Great ships sailed through the marquee with arrangements of roses attached to the rigging and grouped on and around great casks at the base. Displays featuring Flemish flower paintings, the French influence and the Victorian era were well integrated with the overall theme. The competitive floral arrangement reached a high standard, with such titles as 'The Spanish Armada Banquet', a superb exhibit using pewter candlesticks and pewter goblets amid a marvellous selection of well-grouped pink, mauve and crimson flowers on a pink tablecloth over grey, to tone with the pewter. There was even 'The Australian Bicentennial', with Cocos palm spathes depicting the silhouette of the Opera House.

After leaving London we visited Rosemary Verey's lovely garden in the Cotswolds filled with interesting bulbs and perennials, old roses and herbs. It was then on to Hidcote Manor where I found many of the huge bushes of hybrid musks had been removed since my last visit but the border of 'Rosa Mundi' was still good, as was a nice bed of lovely 'Gruss an Aachen' in the white garden. Hidcote was the only garden which had deteriorated since my last visit. The whole garden had an overgrown look.

From the Cotswolds we went to Wales to Powis Castle, my favourite garden in the United Kingdom. The castle is built on a high hill with a series of terraces cascading down the slope. These face south and get all the available sunshine (we hardly saw any in over a month in England) and are planted with an amazing selection of shrubs, bulbs and perennials from all over the world. The plants revel in the well-drained conditions of the steep slope, and the colour-blending was well done. A huge bush of 'Kiftsgate' looked stunning against the subdued red brick of the castle and in a sheltered spot I found the best bush of 'Gloire de Dijon' I had ever seen. The series of terraces led down to a flatter area where roses were well used with herbaceous plants – a border of 'Iceberg' alternating with 'Golden Wings', with gold, silver and white underplantings, was well done, as was a row of the deep pink 'Elmshorn' mixed with white 'Pax' cascading over a wall. A large planting of David Austin roses was most effective. The castle is built on a limestone ridge suitable for plants that like alkaline conditions and the adjoining flatter land is acid and ideal for ericaceous plants.

After visiting Bodnant we dropped in on the opening day of the Lakeland Rose Show, a very impressive event staged under canvas at Kendall. From there we had a day in the Lake District before heading to the west coast of Scotland, visiting Threave Garden and Culzean Castle, both with lovely roses and herbaceous plants in walled gardens protected from the winds of the Atlantic. Old roses look marvellous climbing over mellow brick walls. Roses in Scotland were still in full flower, as they come later than those in England, and colours in the cool climates are particularly rich.

From the West Coast we had several days in Edinburgh, where roses planted on a steep slope in the Princes Street Gardens looked impressive and tuberous begonias were used as bedding plants in full sun. The Edinburgh Royal Botanic Garden was full of interest – in its world-famous rock garden gentians and meconopsis were still covered with brilliant blue flowers, and the great herbaceous border in front of a clipped hedge must surely be the longest in the world.

From Edinburgh we visited Traquair House at Innerleithen in the Scottish Borders local government area. Traquair House is the oldest inhabited house in Scotland – since 1100 – and here 'Mme Hardy', 'New Dawn' and 'Bobbie James' looked superb espaliered against the mellow brick walls. It was noticeable that the paler roses looked best against the walls, the softer tones complementing their colour more attractively than the brighter blooms.

The next stop was Castle Howard, the setting for *Brideshead Revisited*, in North Yorkshire. The old walled rose garden in memory of Lady Cecilia Howard was lovely. A lot of the old roses were past their best but the hybrid perpetual collection was still good, with roses such as 'Charles Lefebvre', 'Eliza Boelle' and 'Baroness Rothschild' flowering well. There was a brave border of tea roses looking surprisingly good under the protection of a wall, and a wonderful use of grey-foliaged plants and blue flowers to tone with the roses. Great groups of *Pyrus salicifolia* with silvery grey foliage were a feature, as were the borders of bourbon roses grown through tall box-like structures to support the lax growth and show off the arching canes festooned with roses.

From York we made our way to London where part of the group departed for home and six of us stayed an extra week. I was lucky enough to stay with Peter Beales in Norfolk and help put up his display at the Royal Sandringham Show, which the Queen Mother always attends. It won a gold medal and really looked effective, staged at various levels against white latticework in front of a black background. Peter presented the Queen Mother with a basket of roses of his own raising.

As I eventually headed for home, images of roses cascading over mellow brick walls remained in my memory, as did the use of silver foliage, spiked and blue flowers skilfully blended in English gardens with clipped hedges as a background and, most of all, the beauty of old trees in England's lovely countryside.

A Tour of French and German Gardens 1993

(Condensed from an article published in *The Australian Rose Annual* 1994, page 59.)

In June 1993 seventeen heritage rose enthusiasts converged on the great old rose city of Lyon to begin a tour of French and German rose gardens, led by the knowledgeable and much-travelled Bill Grant of the United States. Our tour lasted fourteen days, and was packed full of interesting gardens.

At Lyon La Roseraie du Parc de la Tête d'Or was in full flower – a wonderful site near a lake, with beds of modern roses in excellent condition. I have never seen so many brilliant orange roses vying with one another in degrees of fluorescence and clashing alarmingly with nearby bright pinks, purples and mauves. A lovely fence at the end of the garden covered with reddish pink 'American Pillar' had a border of the orange-red floribunda 'Spartan' in front – an amazing combination. Trees, shrubs and perennials and grassed paths through the informal beds made this a most attractive garden. Lyon can be quite hot in the summer and the mass of contrasting colours gave the garden quite a Mediterranean air.

In another part of the immense park was a totally different garden of old roses, with beds of the different classes intermingled with a good collection of climbing roses on supports. The species collection was past its peak but it contained a number of rare varieties, with some gigantic bushes. I was interested in the collection of tea roses, particularly two coppery coloured varieties, 'Mme Emilie Charrin' and 'Souvenir de Gilbert Nabonnand', neither of which I had previously come across.

'Spartan'.
(*Photograph courtesy Margaret Furness*)

One of the highlights of the whole trip was our visit to La Bonne Maison, the garden of Odile and Georges Masquelier, a hectare in area and perched on a steep slope overlooking the rivers Rhone and Saone, where great use of 3 to 5 metre retaining walls has been made to house an incredible collection of climbing roses. This resulted in a series of gardens within a garden, with excellent use of pergolas – there were five of them, some running along the slope, some downslope, and even one going diagonally. They were all clothed with roses in pinks and mauves, soft yellows, pale apricots and, of course, cream and white to give an effect of complete colour harmony. Arches festooned with such rampant growers as 'The Garland', 'Seagull' and 'Bobbie James' covered the entrances to the 'garden room', which contained a marvellous collection of gallicas, mosses, centifolias and bourbons, all in excellent condition with basal growth replacing some of the old wood each year. Two new shrub climbers from Louis Lens, the single white 'Pleine de Grace' and the double white flushed pink 'Dentelle de Malines', were just covered in flowers and a remarkable sight, both here and at Sangerhausen (and again at David Austin's lovely display garden at Albrighton, near Wolverhampton in England). Odile used all sorts of bulbs and perennials among her roses for early and late colour. Her garden will remain in our memories for a long time.

Cascading ramblers in Odile Masquelier's garden overlooking Lyon.

Another quite remarkable garden south of Paris in the little town of Pithiviers is that of nurseryman André Eve. We entered through a gate in the main street, walked down a narrow corridor at the side of the house and came across a glade of roses. Never have I seen such a display of old roses in a small area. Vast climbers were cascading out of trees and supported by forked sticks around the perimeter of the garden to form a background to grass paths just wide enough to walk through. The garden was completely filled with hundreds of old roses and perennial plants. Those of you afraid to grow 'The Garland' and 'Bobbie James' in a small garden, follow André Eve and plant them in trees along the boundaries and you can transform a suburban garden into a woodland glade.

André Eve pointing out a hidden treasure to me in his remarkable garden at Pithiviers. (Sue Zwar behind me is assiduously taking notes.)

The formal rose garden, Bagatelle, was looking excellent on a very hot day. I am always amazed at the use of four bush roses planted round a standard rose – how one does not grow into the other is controlled by ruthless pruning. On leaving this section of the garden, I saw in the distance, across a vast expanse of lawn, what looked like a massive planting of hydrangeas in front of a woodland filled with rhododendrons. On closer scrutiny, the hydrangeas turned out to be a wonderful collection of shrub and ground-cover roses planted in bold groups of one variety. Some of the great English rhododendron gardens could use roses in sunny spots to prolong the flowering season when the rhododendrons have finished.

Next port of call was La Roseraie de l'Haÿ, where 'Alexandre Girault' was looking its best over its great supporting structure, and the alternating pyramids of 'Paul's Scarlet' and 'Mrs F.W. Flight' were as lovely as ever. The collections of hybrid perpetuals, bourbons and spinosissimas were spoiled by hard pruning to ground level – in fact, some bushes had no flowers at all. But it is the climbing roses on the arches, pergolas, tripods and tunnels that are the joy of l'Haÿ, for the pruning is more restrained and the plants can reach their full potential. Truly outstanding were 'Long John Silver' and 'Baltimore Belle', both hybrids of *Rosa setigera*, and 'American Pillar' was stunning. Another interesting feature was the use of hybrid perpetuals pegged down to form a low border 60 centimetres high and flowering all along the stems at the nodes.

From Paris we went by train through glorious countryside to Germany en route to Sangerhausen. The hot weather in France gave way to cool, cloudy conditions which suited both us and the roses. I had been to Sangerhausen in 1983 for their eightieth birthday celebrations and here we were for their ninetieth – and in 2003 I was to join the World Federation of Rose Societies in celebrating their centenary. The accommodation, so spartan in 1983, has improved enormously over time, as have the meals, which were the best we had in Germany. We were escorted round the Rosarium by Deputy Director Frau Brumme, who was interested in our arguments over the naming of some varieties and took notes for future reference. The collection at Sangerhausen is mind-boggling, 6500 varieties in 40 classes – 130 000 bushes in all. Sangerhausen is set in the centre of woodland – an open area where the roses grow. Hybrid teas and floribundas are planted in rows of twelve bushes, very close together, with large areas of one colour planted together to give a harmonious effect. I checked hundreds of varieties of those that I knew and only found a handful wrongly labelled – quite a feat in such a large collection.

But it is the old roses that are such a feature of Sangerhausen. They do not die back from the cold like the moderns and so each bush can reach its full potential. Great beds of centifolias, albas, gallicas et

A grouping of the David Austin roses 'Wise Portia', 'Charles Austin' and 'Cymbeline' at Sangerhausen.

cetera are surrounded by lawn and the bushes cascade down onto the grass to create an incredibly beautiful effect. The use of climbers at Sangerhausen is quite unique. Every two years the larch poles which the climbers are trained on are replaced and the old wood thinned out. The poles are anything from 2 to 6 metres high and the rose is tied closely to the pole to form a very tall, thin pillar. Some of the pillars are only a metre or so apart. The effect of the pale roses against the dark green background of the woodland is magic.

After two full days at Sangerhausen – and even then it was not enough – we went by train to the lovely old city of Kassel, right in the centre of the united Germany. The city is dominated by the castle of Wilhelmshöhe, set in a great park of huge old trees from all over the world. In the park, set amid a rushing stream and several lakes, is the most romantic rose garden I have ever seen. It contains 1600 old roses, many of them gigantic climbers cascading out of trees, and at that time was looked after by Dr and Frau Grimm, both octogenarians, whose knowledge of old roses was quite remarkable. The roses were grouped together in informal beds in the grass, with paths winding through and always the background of water with gigantic tulip trees, ginkgos, elms, oaks and conifers rising up the steep hillsides behind. Great mounds of 'Venusta Pendula', *Rosa multiflora carnea*, *R. arvensis* and 'The Garland' grew up trees and tumbled down to the water, where their pale flowers were reflected beautifully. I was amazed at the number of hips on most of the species roses, which must be a real spectacle in September. To add to my enjoyment I found an excellent collection of the Old Masters in the castle, including Abraham Mignon, Jan Davidzoon de Heem, Rachel Ruysch and Jan van Brueghel.

Our last port of call on this trip was the great Rosarium at Dortmund, which is set in an enormous park with roses being used in every conceivable manner. There was an Edwardian rose bower encircled by ramblers, as well as great use of ground covers, miniatures and weeping roses. It was interesting to see pillar roses cut down to ground level after flowering to encourage new growth for the next year. Dortmund had a very imaginative Director in Dr Bunneman and the garden was constantly changing because of this. I was most interested in a huge area of roses grouped in their countries of origin, but Australia looked a bit sad because a lot of Alister Clark's roses with *Rosa gigantea* blood are not winter hardy in Germany. By my next visit in 1993 this area had disappeared to make way for new gardens.

It was then farewell to the group and off to England to help with the New Zealand Roseworld stand at Hampton Court, but that is another story.

Gardens of the USA 1985
(Condensed from an article published in *The Australian Rose Annual* 1986, page 121.)

On 8 June 1985, I set out with eight other Australians for the seventh World Rose Convention in Toronto. Our first port of call was San Francisco and here we were in the capable hands of the indefatigable Miriam Wilkins and her husband Dick.

We first visited the lovely Berkeley Botanic Gardens perched high on a hill overlooking San Francisco Bay. The garden was divided into sections of plants indigenous to various arid and semi-arid climates of the world, and was of great interest to us. The sheltered areas of very acid soil were planted with rhododendrons and other ericaceous plants and the more exposed areas to a fascinating collection of plants from Mexico and Arizona. The rose garden, though small, was delightful. Beds were bordered with dwarf lavender and the carpets of soft mauve *Verbena peruviana* were a delightful complement to the old roses. A huge bush of 'Mutabilis' caught my eye, as did a wonderful bush of historic 'Soleil d'Or' just smothered in flowers – a most important link with all the flame-coloured roses of today through the Pernetianas. 'Sombreuil' looked enchanting over a wooden pergola. There were huge bushes of richly coloured *Rosa foetida* and *R. foetida lutea* – some of the first of the species to start and the last to finish. The lovely old albas 'Celeste' and 'Maiden's Blush' with their grey foliage were a picture with the mauve verbena in the foreground and a big bush of the gallica 'Président de Sèze', smothered in lilac-pink flowers, completed the scene.

It was then on to Miriam and Dick Wilkins for lunch and a look at their gloriously abundant garden. There were roses everywhere, growing up trees and into shrubs and into one another to give a medley of colour and scent. Not content with growing them in the ground, Miriam had over 300 varieties in pots – watered every third day by Dick. The new buff-pink, quartered and frilly 'Anna Pavlova' from Peter Beales caught my eye, as did an enormous plant of 'Paul's Himalayan Musk', one of Miriam's favourites but new to me. The

'Mutabilis'.
(Photograph courtesy James Young)

rambler 'Chevy Chase' – a cross of *Rosa soulieana* and the polyantha
'Eblouissant' – was magnificent, a fiery bright crimson-red, unusual in
a rambling rose. 'Cerise Bouquet' was good, as was *Rosa macrophylla*
from the Himalayas – just forming myriads of those flagon-shaped
hips that are so attractive in the autumn. The hybrid musk 'Belinda',
like a tall-growing 'Ballerina', looked beautiful with a background of
the rosy-scarlet *Passiflora jamesonii*. 'Pink Grootendorst' had grown
into a mighty bush and 'White Grootendorst' – new to me – was
even lovelier. The cream rambler 'City of York' was most profuse with
its bloom and an archway of 'Dorothy Perkins' was a feature of the
garden. My only regret was that we had arrived on 9 June, when mid
May would have seen the garden in its prime. Still, we would not have
seen the ramblers and late-flowering varieties if we had been earlier.

It was then north to the nursery and garden of Phillip Robinson and
Gregg Lowery at Santa Rosa, a garden in a vineyard area like my own.
The land around Phillip and Gregg's house was planted with a mass
of well-grown bulbs and perennials cascading over the footpaths in
gay profusion and quite delightful. Phillip had a huge bed of pegged-
down hybrid perpetuals and bourbons – quite the best I have ever
seen – each covering a huge area and flowering magnificently along
each cane. New shoots had developed through the centre of each bush
ready for next year. 'Variegata di Bologna', 'Mabel Morrison', 'Frau
Karl Druschki', 'Mme Isaac Pereire', 'Roger Lambelin' and a host of
others outshone any display of climbing hybrid teas I had previously
seen. Phillip and Gregg had a host of moderns as well as the old
gallicas, centifolias and so on, but my interest was in the tea roses in
a big bed. 'Etoile de Lyon' was new to me – a soft and lovely shade
of apricot, rare in roses. 'William R. Smith' – a soft cream and pale
pink, like so many teas – was flowering well. An unusual rose was
'Alliance Franco-Russe', a cream tea, so strongly quartered that the
segments were quite separated. This garden is a huge drawcard for
old rose enthusiasts and the plants were in their prime at the time we
were there.

We then went on to visit Ralph Moore of miniature rose fame. A true
visionary, not only had he managed to breed mossy miniature roses like
'Dresden Doll', 'Strawberry Swirl' and 'Fairy Moss' but he also had some
marvellously mossed floribundas in the pipeline. (Unfortunately, none of
these has ever come on the Australian market).

A day at The Huntington Botanic Gardens was a day to remember.

The cactus garden, the camellia garden, the Shakespeare garden and the water garden will live long in my memory, but it was, of course, the rose garden that was my first priority. Again we were a month late, but I could see the glory that had been.

The three great rose arbours at The Huntington must be wonderful in full bloom. Huge bushes of 'Sombreuil' and 'Souvenir de la Malmaison Cl.' had only a few flowers left and there was not much left on the tea roses. However, I was captivated by 'Louis Philippe d'Angers', a pinky-red, very full China, 'Isabella Sprunt', a lemon-yellow tea, 'Rival de Paestum', an ivory tea, 'Souvenir de Pierre Notting', a deep cream tea, and 'Marie Pavie', a very pale pink polyantha of good form grown as a small hedge and quite lovely. 'Susan Louise', a pale pink tea and grown as a huge bush, was prominent here and elsewhere in America and unknown to us. It is bred from the *Rosa gigantea* hybrid, 'Belle Portugaise'. I had grown the large pink polyantha 'Excellenz von Schubert' for years without knowing what it was. I identified it at The Huntington and this gave me great pleasure. This rose is often confused with 'Gartendirektor Otto Linne', which is very similar.

It was then back up north to see Barbara Cannon at Santa Barbara where she and her husband, Wade, have a gracious old Victorian home and lovely garden. The Australian flag was flying from the garage in our honour, a delightful gesture. Barbara's garden was a sheer delight. The old white house was clothed with a mixture of the old and new – 'Don Juan', 'Handel', 'Sparrieshoop', 'Gloire de Dijon', 'Cl. Cecile Brunner', *Rosa banksiae lutea*, 'Alchemist', 'Susan Louise' again, 'Belle of Portugal' and her sport 'White Belle of Portugal', all looking lovely together. The colour blending in this garden was very well done. The front lawn was bordered with the deep pink rose 'Parade', planted in combination with blue agapanthus, and the central feature was a pillar of warm pink 'Reine Victoria'. There was a very pleasing border of flowers of pink and mauve shades with silver-foliaged plants, enclosed by white stone walls, a gem of a courtyard, all whites and pale yellows with festoons of a white pandorea, a hedge of Australian lillypilly and a bed in which were growing tropical hibiscus, rhododendrons and roses – all happy together at Santa Barbara yet from such a wide climatic range. We lunched California style under a blue and white beach umbrella surrounded by pots of bougainvillea – a very happy occasion.

We then flew to Austin, Texas and spent three delightful days as guests of the Austin Rose Society – Austin is Adelaide's twin city.

During a quick call on Mitzi Van Sant on a hot and humid day, we found a peaceful garden filled with tea roses and noisettes, many named and lots waiting to be named in the future. A feature of Mitzi's garden was a large island bed of old roses out in the street – a great idea. Mitzi's roses looked good but were in between flushes except for a fine 'Mermaid' growing up a tree in the shade.

Shreveport in Louisiana, the home of the American Rose Society and the Gardens of the American Rose Center, was our next port of call. Set in a pine forest, the gardens cover 48 hectares, really a series of small, intimate gardens within a large garden. The old rose area was very well designed with winding paths and a backdrop of pines, but sadly many labels were indecipherable and a lot of the roses had succumbed to a cold burst several years beforehand and had not been replaced. There were, however, good bushes of 'Georg Arends', 'Frau Karl Druschki', 'Reine Victoria' and 'Jacques Cartier', and a good bed of rugosas. 'Mutabilis', as always, was huge and so was *Rosa roxburghii*.

A quick look at Boston and the famous Arnold Arboretum and the James P. Kelleher rose garden where arbours of 'New Dawn' and 'Summer Snow' and 'Paul's Scarlet' were right at their spring peak.

It was then off to Toronto for the Convention, a very well organised, informative and happy affair.

Gardens of New Zealand 1985
(Condensed from an article published in *The Australian Rose Annual* 1986, page 150.)

In December 1985 I visited New Zealand for the Hawera Rose Conference, and viewed many lovely gardens during my stay.

Our first visit was to the Nancy Steen Garden in Auckland, which is beautifully incorporated into the lovely Parnell Rose Gardens, formal in design, but softened like Sissinghurst Castle and Hidcote Manor by the random planting of all sorts of perennial plants and bulbs in soft tonings. The use of grey and silver foliage plants was very well done, and spike flowers like mignonette, foxgloves, campanulas and delphiniums gave excellent contrast in form to the round shapes of the roses.

I found a plant of the rose 'Achievement', growing on lattice-work, quite fascinating. With pink flowers like the polyantha 'The Fairy', its soft cream and green variegated foliage was quite unique, and it was the first of a long list of roses that Deane Ross and I decided we had to import to gardens that were already far too big to manage! (I managed to obtain a plant but the foliage reverted to plain green after several years.) Companion plants chosen for the garden were just perfect – nepeta, *Lychnis coronaria* (I have always called it *Agrostemma*), hostas, hellebores, fascinating green and white nicotiana, dianthus, armeria, bearded iris and white flowered deutzias, and spiraeas and philadelphus, with their arching sprays of flowers, for more contrast.

The pergola at the entrance to the garden will be a lovely feature when it is fully clothed with such beauties as 'Souvenir de la Malmaison Cl.', *Rosa polyantha grandiflora* and 'Mme Alfred Carriere'. As a backdrop to the simple but beautiful white garden, two pink blushed pink roses looked magnificent – 'Blush Rambler' and the slightly darker 'Tausendschön'. Their growth in eighteen months was quite outstanding.

This garden was predominantly whites and pinks and blues and soft crimsons, but a feeling of depth and piquancy was given by bushes of the purple gallicas 'Hippolyte', 'Violacea', 'Tuscany' and 'Sissinghurst Castle', and the mauve-purple 'Belle de Crécy', 'Anais Ségalas' and 'Cardinal de Richelieu'.

The garden is a wonderful tribute to Mrs Steen, who was such a pioneer in fostering the love of heritage roses, not only in New Zealand but also throughout the world.

Our next port of call in Auckland was Toni Sylvester's garden. I had been there once before, in September, when very few roses were out, so I had some idea what was in store for me and I was not disappointed. There were roses cascading everywhere, growing up huge pine trees, over old stumps, through trees and shrubs, all mingling together with a most harmonious and carefully chosen collection of perennials and bulbs and interesting foliage plants. Huge clumps of sisyrinchium, yellow spikes of wachendorfia and lovely white hibiscus-like lavatera caught my eye.

Tea roses were in excellent condition – my old favourite, the light pink, thornless 'G. Nabonnand' (known incorrectly for many years as 'Jean Ducher') was there, with softest apricot 'Mme Falcot' and rich pink, flat and quartered 'Mrs B.R. Cant'. The late flowering floribunda 'Mrs Inge Poulsen', in softest pink was very lovely, but it was the ramblers and climbers that really fascinated me – no hard pruning here, but allowed to develop to the full and show their natural grace. 'Evangeline' was a joy to behold, growing on a wooden support and showing its 8 centimetre single, softest pink flowers with golden stamens to perfection. Toni warned me of the mildew later on, but it was added to the list! 'Laure Davoust', a very pale pink rambler, was gorgeous and new to me, as was 'René André', buff yellow in bud opening to pale pink, flushed deeper pink in clusters. The rambler 'May Queen', which I have grown for many years because of its unusual soft lilac-pink colour and lovely flat quartered form, was looking great. It is equally at home growing up a tree or cascading down a bank or used as a ground cover. The hybrid musk 'Mme d'Arblay', with its huge clusters of softest flesh pink, smallish flowers, was also new to me, while 'Dundee Rambler' brought back memories of the pergola festooned with this amazing soft cream rose at Nancy Steen's garden in 1971 – a sight I will never forget. It was later removed, unfortunately, because of the work involved in keeping it in check.

Next we went to June Bell's lovely garden with its sense of spaciousness. Huge bushes of old roses with plenty of room to spread were a sight to behold. The picturesque old white wooden house was clothed on one side with a bush of 'Wedding Day' trained along a veranda; its huge trusses of white flowers with golden stamens looked perfect with its foil of rich green leaves against the white house. 'Bloomfield Courage' was there too, but I was surprised to find that, gorgeous as it was, it did not appeal like 'Wedding Day'.

June had an intriguing sport of the gallica 'Camaieux'. Instead of a pale pink background with rose-mauve stripes, the flowers had masses of small imbricated petals of pale pink, dotted and marbled with rosy-mauve. It was different from any other gallica I have ever seen. We gave it the name "Camaieux Fimbriata".

We were loath to leave Auckland with its amazing gardens and friendly guides, but it was off in a huge bus – all eight of us – to Hawera and the first World Heritage Rose Convention.

The gardens we visited as part of the convention were marvellous. We just drooled over the rich, black volcanic soil in Taranaki – hundreds of feet of it in places, all that rainfall and an ample supply of cow and sheep manure – what more could one ask for!

Our first garden was that of Mr and Mrs Watts at Patea – an interesting farm garden incorporating a lot of modern roses with old ones, and an excellent lot of vegetables. 'Ripples', a deep mauve floribunda, was quite outstanding as were some climbing roses at the back of the house.

Next was King Edward Park at Hawera. The park contained a broad collection of old roses protected from gales from the sea by a good windbreak. A pergola was well clothed with climbing roses, among which 'Constance Spry' was outstanding. There were some excellent bourbons too, including 'Great Western', 'Mme Ernst Calvat' and 'Mme Isaac Pereire'.

I will always remember Trevor and Del Simpson's garden at Tariki. Not only did it contain an enormous collection of modern roses of all types, but also an amazing collection of old roses, lightly pruned and set in informal beds in the lawn. They were the best-grown collection of old roses I have seen anywhere – soil, rainfall, abundant cow and sheep manure, well sprayed and plenty of tender loving care certainly had produced results. I remember stopping at the most enormous blooms of 'Charles de Mills' and asking, 'Can it really be you?'

A visit to Mr and Mrs Josephson's garden showed just how well rhododendrons could be featured in shady spots with roses in sunny areas. The curved drive into this meticulously cared for garden was very well designed and all roses, hybrid teas, floribundas and miniatures, were in excellent condition.

A similar garden to the Josephsons' was that of Margaret Chapman-Taylor, a garden that had a look of Wisley or Savill – praise indeed! The sweeps of lawn and heavily planted curved beds with an enormous variety of choice trees, shrubs and climbing plants, bulbs and perennials made a huge garden comparatively easy to maintain.

The Hollards' rhododendron garden at Kaponga must be one of New Zealand's greatest gardens. The rhododendrons and azaleas were magnificent, and Asiatic primulas, hostas and other shade-loving plants revelled in the rich soil and protection from lovely old trees. On the drive a huge specimen bush of *Rosa moyesii* caught my eye. It is indigenous to the Himalayas and was really at home here, ablaze with its single red flowers with lovely stamens – and what a sight it must be when in hip in the autumn. This was a fitting climax to a wonderful week in wonderful gardens with wonderful people in a wonderful country.

Gardens of Italy 1999

In my many trips to Europe looking at roses and gardens with groups of like-minded people I have found that there has been more enthusiasm for gardens in Italy than any other country – except, perhaps, for the United Kingdom. I think this might be because in Italy with its Mediterranean climate we are able to recognise many of the plants that will survive hot dry summers. We can also appreciate famous gardens which date back hundreds of years and are perfect foils for ancient buildings and mellow old walls. The other element is the music of running water from streams, in cascades, fountains and lakes.

The tour I organised to Italy in 1999 included many unique gardens.

The garden of Maresa del Bufalo in the outskirts of Rome had a huge range of roses, many of them climbers growing up the magnificent trees scattered around the extensive grounds. They clambered through copper beeches, birches, tulip trees and ornamental fruit trees, cascading downwards with wild abandon. I think that out of the hundred or so trees growing in the garden, ninety-eight of them would have been supporting a rose. Although I can speak no Italian and Maresa's English is negligible we seemed to speak the same language – that of roses. As we were leaving one of the group asked me how long I had known our hostess, to which I replied, 'Two hours, the same as you have!'

Another garden near Rome was La Landriana, which was designed by an Englishman, Russell Page. Here there were exciting contrasts between various areas. The long straight entrance had hundreds of 'Bonica' roses planted among olive trees which had been pruned to show their interesting, gnarled old trunks. This led to a series of very formal parterres around the house. The most spectacular contained rows of rounded domes of sour orange trees clipped into shape with an underplanting of small clipped conifers. From the house, framed by a huge pergola planted with wisteria, jasmine and roses, we walked down to a lake surrounded by banks of very well-grown old roses in huge informal drifts. The contrast between this and the formal areas was brilliant. To top it all off there was a sloping grove of olive trees interspersed with three hundred shrubs of 'Mutabilis' with their single flowers that change from yellow to salmon to crimson, looking like a flight of butterflies from a distance.

I had met Professor Gianfranco Fineschi on numerous occasions at World Federation of Rose Societies conferences, where I had discovered that he was probably the most knowledgeable rose

The charming Maresa del Bufalo, describing a plant to me.

An enormous climbing 'Mlle Cecile Brunner' swallowing a summerhouse in Maresa del Bufalo's garden.

The pale apricot-pink noisette, 'Jaune Desprez', is only one of the many climbers trained into trees by Maresa del Bufalo.

lover in the world. Born in 1923, he graduated from the faculty of medicine at the University of Florence, specialising in orthopaedics and traumatology, and went on to become professor at the famous Vatican University of the Sacred Heart in Rome until he retired in 1997. He was also the Pope's doctor. His garden is on the family property at Cavriglia in the Chianti wine growing area, about 45 kilometres south of Florence, and it has been a huge drawcard for rose lovers from all over the world.

The garden contains a bush of each of over 7000 varieties. Climbers give height. They are grown on poles – wooden, stone and metal structures – and cascade downwards. Paths dissect the garden with more height obtained by 3 metre standards of hybrid teas and floribundas. There are beds of all the old rose classes with magnificent gallicas, centifolias, mosses, albas, damasks, hybrid perpetuals and bourbons. All the famous rose breeders are recognised with vast collections of their introductions and there is also a collection for roses bred in specific countries of the world. Above all, if you asked Professor Fineschi about a rose, he would know its parentage, date of release and breeder. He had an encyclopaedic memory. This is not a garden of sweeping lawns and trees but a world collection of roses, the life interest of a brilliant man. The highlight of our day was a special lunch under a pergola at the back of the home served with wine made on the property. (Sadly, Professor Fineschi died in 2010 at the age of 93. His funeral service was conducted in the garden and attended by thousands. His sister and three daughters wish to maintain this priceless collection of roses as a tribute to this amazing man).

Professor Fineschi's immaculate rose garden, the world's largest private collection of roses.

'Trier', the founder of the Reverend Joseph Pemberton's hybrid musk roses, growing in Professor Fineschi's garden.

Another unique garden we visited was that of Walter Branchi at Orieto, on a lake north of Rome in mountainous country. I had always wanted to visit Walter's famous collection of teas, Chinas and noisettes and I managed this on a very wet day. We were amazed at the quality of the teas in particular. They were pruned hard in the winter and were the largest and best formed I had ever seen. From his catalogue I counted sixty-seven varieties I had never seen before. The clay soil had been dug over – and I remember being hosed down from toes to thighs after I slipped while trying to take close-up photographs of rose blooms.

I have left my favourite garden till last. This is Ninfa, 70 kilometres south-east of Rome, defined by many as an earthly paradise. The town of Ninfa was built in 1297 by the Caetani family but in a civil war in 1382 it was destroyed, along with its seven churches and massive castle tower. It remained a ruin because of the constant recurrence of malaria from the mosquito-infected Pontine marshes nearby (which were not drained until the early twentieth century). The buildings slowly decayed and became overgrown by native vegetation until Duke Onorato Caetani and his English wife Ada decided to restore the garden in the 1880s. Among the first roses they planted were *Rosa moschata*, 'Mme Alfred Carriere', 'Maréchal Niel' and 'Alister Stella Grey', and 'General Schablikine', which is planted in groups around the garden. Water was introduced, with interweaving fast-running streams crossing over rocks and ponds filled with arum lilies, water iris and giant gunnera. Roses cascade into the water where their flowers are reflected. A hedge of *Rosa roxburgii plena* near the entrance is a major feature of the garden, as is a long wall completely covered with climbing roses. However, it is the ancient ruins of the churches that give the garden its serene but magic quality. Climbing roses cover the walls and cascade downwards but are carefully trimmed to make sure that the ruins remain dominant.

The duke's niece, Lelia Caetani, the last surviving member of the great and very wealthy Caetani family, married Hubert Howard, an Englishman, and they kept on planting and developing the area.

'The Garland', with 'Paul's Himalayan Musk', two of many huge ramblers reaching high into an Italian cypress at Ninfa

Ramblers along the wall at the entrance to Ninfa.

She used to spend a lot of time especially working in her wildflower meadow, and had a great knowledge of plants. Lelia said she was a custodian of the garden and in 1972 she set up the Roffredo Caetani Foundation in memory of her father to ensure the garden's survival.

The garden's climate is mild, with frost-free winters and summer temperatures up to 37° C. Flowers are everywhere but they never compete with the old ruins and massive old trees. There are many areas for serene contemplation, especially in the cherry collection planted in rough grass studded with spring bulbs. The garden with its mystic quality is unique for its ruins, its views over the dry mountains in the distance, its use of running water, its amazing collections of plants and its subtle blending of colours both in flowers and foliage. It is surely a paradise on earth.

The dominating castle ruin at Ninfa.

Chapter 7

Articles from the Past

Roses under Irrigation
(Condensed from the first article I wrote for any rose journal, published in *The Australian and New Zealand Rose Annual* 1959, page 105.)

For many years roses have been the most popular of garden plants in the Murray Valley, due to their long flowering period, their freedom from pests and diseases, and the ease with which they can be grown in this warm, dry climate.

Rose gardens under irrigation can be divided into those under flood irrigation and those under spray irrigation. My entire rose garden of about 1400 plants is flood-irrigated roughly every fourteen days in the summer. I find that roses do extremely well under this system, and keep a continuous display of blooms from late September, when *Rosa laevigata* first appears, right up to pruning time in early August. We are particularly fortunate in being able to enjoy excellent blooms in the winter months from such varieties as 'Texas Centennial', 'President Herbert Hoover', 'Radiance', 'Hector Deane' and 'Lorraine Lee'.

The soil in the region varies considerably, from pure red sand to very heavy clay. The soil in my rose garden is a rich clay loam that holds water very well. However, roses in the Murray Valley also do well on sandy soil providing they are watered frequently. Quite a few of the gardens on sandy soil are under spray irrigation – there is a disadvantage to spray irrigation, however, in that it causes full blooms to flop, which can spread mildew and black spot.

I usually find that the best time to prune is in early August, as the plants are most dormant during that time and the canes have had time to fully mature. I am an advocate of light pruning, as I consider heavy pruning seriously affects plant vigour.

'President Herbert Hoover'.
(Photograph courtesy James Young)

Our first flush of bloom usually comes in mid October followed by a second, more fleeting flush in late November and early December. By the time the last of the late-flowering floribundas, ramblers and varieties like 'Frau Karl Druschki' and 'Mermaid' have finished their first flush, early-blooming varieties like 'Picture', 'Golden Emblem' and 'President Herbert Hoover' have started on their second flush, so we are never really short of roses.

Of course, in the middle of summer hot northerly winds can cause a lot of scorching, but even in the hottest weather good blooms can be seen each morning before the temperature rises.

Usually I give the roses a good manuring of four parts blood and bone, two parts sulphate of ammonia, two parts superphosphate and one part sulphate of potash in the first week of March to ensure a good crop of flowers in April and May. This manuring is sufficiently stimulating for Renmark soils to produce another crop of blooms during the winter – although, of course, it is by no means as plentiful as the autumn crop.

As far as pests and diseases are concerned, because of our dry atmosphere we have little trouble from black spot or mildew. The average annual rainfall is only 9 inches (230 mm), although I consider our plants under irrigation would receive something like 60 or 70 inches (1500–1800 mm). Aphids are troublesome at times, but I find our supply of birds keeps the aphid population very low. Thrips can be very bad in the spring. In fact, this year [1958] they have been in plague proportions for weeks, owing to the continuance of cool weather. I have sprayed a number of times but some of the whites, pale pinks and buff yellows are still marked. Light brown apple-moth has caused quite a lot of damage. The small green grubs of the moth eat through the bud and, of course, ruin the flower. Usually I spray for mildew twice in the spring and twice in the autumn as a precautionary measure. I spray for black spot only during any prolonged rain during summer, a very rare occurrence.

My preferred rootstock by far is *Rosa indica major*, which I find much stronger than *R. multiflora*. The plants on *R. indica major* are at least twice the size of those on *R. multiflora*, they do not scorch so much in the hot weather and they also come into growth far more quickly after flowering. Oddly, the difference between the two stocks does not seem as pronounced on floribundas as it does on hybrid teas. I also found that when the garden was inundated to a depth of 6 to 18 inches (15–45 cm) for a fortnight during the great flood of 1956, fifty of the seventy-five roses that died were on *R. multiflora*.

I like to plant with the bud union just below ground level. This prevents sunscald to the union and helps prevent rocking in windy weather. The only disadvantage of deep planting is that weeds can be troublesome among the basal shoots.

Under most of my roses there is a ground cover of various perennial plants. I think it is important to have a ground cover to prevent the sun's rays reaching the soil and to prevent evaporation from wind. The ground cover helps to smother most weeds and also obviates the need for constant tilling of the soil.

Shrub Roses Old and New

(Condensed from an article published in *The Australian and New Zealand Rose Annual*
1962, page 53.)

My interest in shrub roses was aroused about five or six years ago. I had procured the Kordes hybrid varieties 'Berlin', 'Bonn' and 'Grandmaster' and planted them along an irrigation channel where they thrived. Their flowering was so spectacular that I decided to try more varieties. These too thrived and it was then that I realised just how fascinating a hobby I had started – a journey, as it were, into the realm of roses of the past. I became so engrossed in the characteristic features of the gallicas, albas, damasks and centifolias that I now have a thriving plantation of nearly three hundred varieties planted as a border to our turfed fruit-drying area. New additions are planted each year, the result of collecting buds from specimens seen while travelling during vacations.

Visitors who are interested in roses invariably start making enquiries when they see the old roses in bloom. It does not take them long to notice that 'Cardinal de Richelieu' and 'Nuits de Young' are far more purple and conspicuous than any of the so-called blue moderns. 'Careless Love' is bypassed when such striking varieties of striped roses as 'Camaieux', 'Tricolore de Flandre' and 'Variegata de Bologna' come into view. But I think that one of the main features of the old roses that attracts so many people is the exotic perfume. This quality is really lacking in so many of the moderns whereas in the old roses, whether they be damask, alba, centifolia or gallica, it is intense and lasting.

Some people take quite a long time to appreciate the form of the old roses. They still have their minds on the high pointed bud of the moderns but when they look closely into the heart of a bloom such as 'Mme Hardy', with its delicate folds and central green eye, they soon realise that here is a beauty of form of a different type altogether.

As far as culture is concerned, old roses literally grow themselves. Occasionally aphids or mildew attack them but I think that they would probably get along just as well without any spraying. I believe in planting the bush with the bud union below ground level so that they can produce their own roots in addition to those of the stock. The gallicas, in particular, when on their own roots like to form thickets. I prefer to give old roses a light pruning to improve the length of stem and quality of flowers; weak canes are shortened back approximately to half and strong vigorous canes are twisted around each other to give a basket effect.

'Mme Hardy'.
(Photograph courtesy Billy West)

Regarding varieties, there are so many that are really beautiful that it is a real problem to make a choice. The oldest varieties, the gallicas, are sturdy though somewhat dwarf shrubs of compact habit, and flower only in spring. The alba varieties are distinguished by their grey-green foliage, rather large hooked thorns and vigorous spreading habit of growth. All make charming large shrubs, and flower only in spring. Of the damasks my favourite is 'Mme Hardy', which is a tall bush 6–7 feet (1.8–2 m) high with soft green foliage and wonderful camellia-like blooms of pure white with an incurved centre and a green eye. The beauty of this rose is enhanced by its pale pink buds. The perfume is superlative, a truly outstanding rose. There is also a wonderful variety of centifolias to choose from.

From the more modern-looking bourbons we get some recurrent bloom. These roses seem to combine the foliage of the China roses with the sumptuous colouring and striping of the old varieties. The cupped form of the flowers of the bourbons is also derived from the Chinas. Many are climbing in habit.

Passing on to the noisettes, we are approaching the tea rose in form, scent and colour. Most are climbing varieties and all are as recurrent as any modern hybrid tea. The blood of the musk rose is evident in most of the noisettes. I still also have a soft spot for a small group of old roses, the hybrid perpetuals.

Having dealt with the biggest of the groups of old roses, I feel that mention must be made of some of the species and their hybrids, which are so charming. Firstly that great old evergreen climber, *Rosa laevigata*, the best rose I know of for a screen. Its wonderful glossy green foliage has never had an atom of disease and its purest white single blooms with golden stamens have wonderful substance. It is the first rose to bloom in the early spring and one of the best. The pink form 'Anemone' has not the substance, lasts a very short time and is addicted to mildew. However, the form 'Ramona' is a wonderful rose of the richest pink with none of the failings of its parent ('Anemone'), a truly glorious variety that is hardly surpassed by any other single pink rose. *Rosa bracteata* is another evergreen species rose that makes a good screen. Its plump buds in their leafy casing are charming and the single cream flowers with golden stamens are very beautiful. This rose is inclined to layer whenever it touches the ground. Even more lovely is its offspring, 'Mermaid', that single beauty with golden stamens. Even when the petals drop the stamens are still lovely. Would that all modern roses would clean themselves so well.

The banksia roses should be more widely grown for the beauty of foliage, scent and early flowers. The double white banksia rose is just as lovely as the yellow. Also, the wonderful *Rosa* x *fortuneana*, a hybrid from *R. banksiae*, has double white flowers like large peach blooms, borne singly along the stems for months.

Rosa davidii, with its ferny foliage, single pink flowers in small clusters and bright scarlet autumn hips, is a very fine species indeed. Lovely too is 'Dupontii', that cross between the musk rose and a gallica, with white single flowers that have lovely golden stamens, a beautifully formed, single spring-flowering rose that is outstanding in its simplicity. Grey foliage adds to the effect.

Rosa foetida bicolor.
(Photograph courtesy Marianne Wakelin)

In our hot climate the foetida group is magnificent. *Rosa foetida bicolor* or 'Austrian Copper' forms a big bush and the single brilliant copper-red flowers with yellow reverse make a really dazzling display. The yellow form, *R. foetida lutea*, is also very appealing but not as eye-catching as the former. Another dazzling display can be had from the double 'Persian Yellow', its yellow colour so intense that it brightens the whole planting of the old roses. First of the species roses to flower is *R. hugonis*, with its single clear yellow blooms on long arching sprays. It and *R. primula*, the incense rose, both have fern-like foliage and clear yellow flowers.

I have found that the incomparable *Rosa moyesii* and its hybrids need shade or the fruits will burn before reaching maturity. The lovely red blooms of *R. moyesii* with their golden stamens are a sheer delight, and the display of bottle-shaped red hips is magnificent in the winter. *R. nitida* with its shining green leaves, single bright pink flowers and red hips, is a good little rose for the front of a border. It always looks neat and attractive. *Rosa pseudo-indica* or 'Fortune's Double Yellow' must be mentioned because of its striking buff salmon-orange blooms – a very modern colour for an old rose. *Rosa omeiensis pteracantha* always attracts attention for its huge red translucent thorns. Pruned hard each winter, its long new shoots are fascinating. The burr rose, *R. roxburghii*, with its fat bristly buds that could easily be mistaken for a type of Noogoora burr, is very interesting, and *R. rubrifolia* must find a place because of its rich reddish purple foliage on smooth arching shoots. It is always in keen demand by floral artists.

Well named is 'Wedding Day', a hybrid of *Rosa sinowilsonii*, raised in 1950 by Sir Frederick Stern. The November display of myriad small white single blooms in large clusters is enhanced by the golden stamens. A delightfully fragrant rose that fills in a dull period when many roses have finished their first flush.

All the old rugosa varieties are indispensible with their beautiful foliage, flowers and fruit. They are especially intriguing in the autumn when their flowers and fruit appear together with the rich burnished yellow of the dying foliage.

Before passing on to the modern shrub roses, I must mention the delicately scented old hybrid musk roses, all of which flower continuously through spring to autumn in good-sized clusters and are of delicate colouring, with blooms a little like the 'Ophelia' group. The best, I think, are coppery pink 'Cornelia', salmon 'Felicia', cream 'Pax', the creamy white 'Prosperity', and the incomparable palest pink 'Penelope'. A mixture of these varieties would make a lovely informal hedge in many gardens.

'Ophelia'.
(Photograph courtesy Margaret Furness)

Now to that excellent group of modern shrub roses, most of which are the fruits of the German family of breeders, Kordes. These shrub roses mostly grow to a height of 6–7 feet (1.8–2 m) and are quite indispensible for background effect in large gardens. Almost all are recurrent and flower most of the year. The exceptions are the lovely 'Frühlingsmorgen' ('Spring Morning'), a clear pink beauty paling to yellow in the centre with a core of maroon stamens. The few flowers produced in the autumn are of unsurpassed beauty. The large red to black hips of this variety are also striking. 'Frühlingsgold' ('Spring

'Sparrieshoop'.
(Photograph courtesy Marianne Wakelin)

Gold'), a semi-double, clear soft creamy yellow, is almost as beautiful as the former. 'Sparrieshoop', a clear apple-blossom pink variety that flowers in huge clusters, is one of the most spectacular plants in the spring garden. Surely this must be one of the loveliest single roses in existence. It also blooms continuously. 'Heidelberg', a bright scarlet variety, flowers in small clusters and has lovely form in the bud. I have had it only two years but am very impressed. 'Florence Mary Morse', a semi-double scarlet, is the most free-flowering red rose one could imagine. It flowers non-stop from October to July and has that happy habit of flowering on laterals before the central cluster is finished. 'Elmshorn', a bright pink variety, is superb in the autumn when its flowers deepen to almost a red. 'Berlin' is a wonderful grower, producing enormous clusters of single orange-scarlet roses that put to shame any floribunda for the size of truss. 'Iceberg' (released in 1958 as 'Schneewittchen' or 'Snow Witch'), and now classified as a floribunda, is really a shrub rose. It produces many times more flowers than any other white rose. In fact, a few days ago I estimated roughly five hundred blooms and buds on one three-year-old plant. The bud form is perfection in itself and the fully opened blooms with their yellow stamens are delightful. This is easily one of the greatest roses of this century in our climate.

I must mention two shrub roses produced by Mr Riethmuller of Sydney. Firstly, 'Titian', which is an amazing flowerer of a colour little less vivid than 'Montezuma', with a quartered centre common in the old roses – a grand Australian rose. There is also 'Spring Song', a tall shrub with beautiful foliage that flowers well here in huge rose-pink sprays in mid winter.

I am afraid that I have not been able to mention here all the varieties I would have liked to and also I have not grown quite a few of the promising varieties long enough to estimate their value in this climate. However, I hope that more and more people will realise the value of these old varieties, which need so little attention, and that they will learn to appreciate their beauty of form, their velvety softness and above all their exquisite fragrance. Perhaps we might gain a little more peace in this hurried existence of ours if sometimes we turn our thoughts for a short while to those old roses of a more leisurely era.

'Titian'.
(Photograph courtesy Margaret Furness)

Overture and Finale of Spring

(Written as Vice-President of the SA Rose Society; condensed from an article published in
The Australian and New Zealand Rose Annual 1963, page 79.)

As I write this at home in Renmark in South Australia's Upper Murray, the spring rose flush is nearly over. The date is November 8, and we can look back on five weeks of good roses. Owing to the very cool October, the roses have flowered for a much longer period than usual and the quality has been excellent.

However, I do not wish to write about those varieties that bloom with the spring flush, but rather those most useful kinds that give us blooms before or after the main flush – in other words, those that bloom in September or November. I must mention that the dates given in this article apply to the early warm areas of South Australia, northern Victoria and western New South Wales, and considerable allowances will have to be made for cooler climates. Of course, the spring flush of bloom can vary over more than a fortnight from year to year also, depending on seasons.

Now let us discuss the first roses of spring, the harbingers of what is to come.

I cannot understand why *Rosa laevigata* is not grown more. Surely it must rank as one of the most beautiful of all single roses and it makes such a wonderful big plant that is quite evergreen and immune

A simple arrangement using *Rosa laevigata*.
(Photograph courtesy Richard Fewster)

to any disease. From the end of August to the first week of October, *R. laevigata* covers itself with large single white cupped blooms with golden stamens that are the very essence of spring in their fresh simplicity.

Opening also in early September are the various forms of *Rosa spinosissima*, the Burnet roses, mostly in creams and soft pinks with lovely stamens. They form small thickets on their own roots and have dainty, ferny foliage, charming flowers and jet black hips in the autumn. A spinosissima hybrid called 'Stanwell Perpetual' is a lovely soft pink colour, very double with quilled central petals and opening flat, and is in flower almost all the year. It is particularly fine in the latter half of September. Several hybrids of *R. spinosissima* raised by Kordes are absolutely essential for early colour in the rose garden. All form big bushes, 6–7 feet (1.8–2 m) high and as much across, and for the whole of September are as spectacular as any shrub one could wish for. 'Frühlingsmorgen' ('Spring Morning'), with its exquisite 4 inch (10 cm) single pink flowers shaded yellow around the centre, and with the most glorious maroon coloured stamens, must rank as probably the loveliest of all single shrub roses. 'Frühlingsgold' ('Spring Gold') is a soft semi-double creamy yellow with deep yellow stamens and has a glorious scent. It is most spectacular in full flower. 'Frühlingsduft' ('Spring Fragrance') certainly lives up to its name with semi-double, deliciously fragrant flowers of creamy pink. 'Frühlingsanfang' ('Spring Beginning'), of a soft ivory colour, is no less pleasing. Its single flowers open very flat.

'Frühlingsmorgen' ('Spring Morning').

'Frühlingsgold' ('Spring Gold').

Mention must be made of *Rosa hugonis*, a great spreading bush with lovely ferny foliage and an abundance of single soft yellow blooms.

Most people know *Rosa foetida bicolor*, the Austrian copper rose. On a rather gaunt bush it produces in September and early October single flowers of coppery red so intense that it has never been equalled by any modern rose. *Rosa foetida lutea* is a dazzling clear yellow that is unique among single roses and the double *R. foetida persiana* has an amazingly long flowering period of five to six weeks in September and early October. In our hot dry climate its intense yellow colour never fades – would that the same could be said for yellow hybrid teas. 'Agnes', a variety produced from a cross between *R. rugosa* and *R. foetida persiana*, makes a wonderful showing in September when its prickly stems are covered with soft yellow blooms that are shaded with amber, often quartered and deliciously scented.

The banksia roses are also at their best in September. Most people love the yellow banksia rose for its soft colour, but what of *R. banksiae alba* with its wonderful perfume of violets? And *R.* x *fortuneana* with its myriad 2 inch (5 cm) creamy white quartered blooms all along the arching canes – a perfect early rose for wired work?

And last of the early roses, but by no means least, we must include the late Alister Clark's *Rosa gigantea* hybrids. 'Harbinger' and 'Courier', both soft pink singles, reach their peak in September after flowering quite well in July and August, as do 'Flying Colours', a rich rose pink, and the peerless cerise 'Nancy Hayward', whose wonderful

'Frühlingsanfang' ('Spring Beginning').

'Frühlingsduft' ('Spring Fragrance'), another of the *Rosa spinosissima* hybrids raised by Kordes.

colour and long flowering period has endeared her to many rosarians. The middle of September usually brings forth Alister Clark's 'Doris Downes', a two-toned rich pink climber that has excellent decorative qualities and well-shaped buds.

In the last week of September in most seasons we can enjoy the first few blooms on such early hybrid teas and climbers as 'Golden Emblem', 'Flaming Sunset', 'Picture', 'Brazil' and 'Black Boy'. Then October brings forth such a spate of varieties that we must pass them by in this article. Of our three thousand bushes, all but two hundred or so reach their peak in October.

However, as the first week of November comes to an end, we look to late-flowering varieties that will give us colour while the hybrid teas and floribundas make new growth before their second flush of bloom in December.

These roses that flower late can be roughly divided into three groups. Firstly the species, then the old-fashioned roses and last the ramblers.

Of the species, *Rosa bracteata* stands out. On an enormous thorny bush it produces vast quantities of single creamy white flowers with lovely golden stamens from November to June. This rose is truly evergreen and is justly famous as the parent of the incomparable 'Mermaid', another tremendous grower with flowers of soft yellow showing a large boss of golden stamens that make it a rose of peerless beauty.

Rosa bracteata.

Mention must be made of *Rosa moschata*, a huge grower which produces enormous quantities of small single cream flowers with golden stamens in large panicles that scent the air for yards around with a delicious musk scent; of *R. davidii*, with soft grey foliage, small rose-pink single flowers that produce lovely scarlet hips in the autumn; of *R. macrantha*, a great sprawling bush laden with lovely single ivory blooms faintly tinged with blush; of *R.* 'Dupontii', a peerless single white flower of perfect rounded form and fruity fragrance; of *R. gallica complicata*, with its myriad deep pink single blooms with golden stamens on a huge plant that produces an amazing display of hips in the autumn; of *R. paulii*, a sprawling ground-covering prickly shrub with starry white flowers, and its pink form, *R. paulii rosea*, whose rich pink blooms shading to soft creamy pink in the centre and golden stamens are delightful; and lastly of the incomparable *R. moyesii* 'Geranium', which is a blazing fiery red colour. A cross between *R. moyesii* and *R. willmottiae*, called *R. hillieri*, has single flowers of dark red shadings that are unique among single roses. These last roses are, if anything, even more spectacular in the autumn when laden with their fiery scarlet bottle-shaped fruit.

By the end of the first week in November a lot of the old gallicas, centifolias, albas, mosses and damasks are past their best but there are some varieties that are a little later and are therefore very welcome. Of the gallicas, pride of place must go to 'Camaieux', a superb rosy-lilac bloom striped heavily with softest pink – probably the most fascinating of all striped roses. 'Rosa Mundi', or *R. gallica versicolor*, with its wonderfully striped blooms, also commands attention. Fortunately there are several late-blooming alba varieties too. 'Celeste', with its lovely scrolled buds of soft pink and exquisite soft pink blooms among grey foliage, is always eagerly awaited, as is the slightly larger 'Great Maiden's Blush', while 'Königin von Dänemark', with its red buds opening to soft pink quartered blooms with button eyes, can only be equalled by the peerless white damask, 'Mme Hardy'.

Of the noisettes that bloom late, I am particularly impressed with 'Alister Stella Gray', with its huge panicles of soft yellow to cream quill-petalled flowers on a plant that blooms from November to July, and 'Aimée Vibert', the last rose of all to flower for me, with huge trusses of white flowers that scent the air for metres about.

The old hybrid perpetual 'Frau Karl Druschki', which is now classified as a hybrid tea – quite wrongly, in my opinion – is a

'Frau Karl Druschki'
(Photograph courtesy Margaret Furness)

wonderful standby in November. This old warrior has been growing by the house for thirty years and still outshines any other white variety for purity of colour and vigour of growth.

Of course the hybrid China 'Bloomfield Abundance' ('Spray Cecile Brunner') is well known for its late-blooming properties, but few people grow 'Perle d'Or' with its lovely soft apricot buds of perfect form. As old as these varieties are, they have never been surpassed for their beauty of bud.

There are a few hybrid teas and floribundas that flower late enough to be included in this article. 'The Texan', a bright red tall-growing hybrid tea, is always reliable, as are the floribundas 'Poulsen's Delight', a single apple-blossom pink that is most spectacular although sorely neglected, 'Florence Mary Morse', a tall-growing and amazingly free-flowering scarlet, 'Orange Triumph', the deep red 'Red Cap', and the very late red Kordes variety 'Ama'.

Last of all I must mention the ramblers. Pride of place must go to 'Francis E. Lester' with its huge clusters of apple-blossom pink blooms amid the small red hips that have persisted right through the winter. 'Bloomfield Courage', a single red with yellow stamens, is always showy. The three mauve ramblers that always command attention are the soft blue-mauve 'Veilchenblau', the rosy-mauve 'Rose Marie Viaud' and the most striking deep violet 'Violette'. 'Silver Moon', a single cream rambler that has great charm when the blooms open from their spiral buds to show golden stamens, is a wonderful grower with good glossy foliage. 'New Dawn', of the softest pink, flowers for the rest of the season. All these ramblers are so vastly superior to 'Dorothy Perkins', who seems to have been born with mildew. And last of all but by no means least the *Rosa sinowilsonii* hybrid 'Wedding Day', so aptly named when covered with its myriad soft yellow flowers that turn to white as they age and show exquisite golden stamens. This wonderful rose will scent the whole neighbourhood with a strange mixture of ripe fruit and musk.

It is interesting to realise just how many of the roses I have mentioned are single. Do we love the first single roses of spring because in their freshness and simplicity they are the very essence of spring? And do we enjoy the single roses of November because they are so simple and unsophisticated after the wealth of large, florid, highly coloured varieties that our eyes have feasted on in October?

Thus it can be seen that with a little bit of planning we can have a spring flush of roses that lasts from early September until early December, by which time the second flush of varieties are in full flower and we have bridged the gap between the first and second flushes of our modern hybrid teas and floribundas.

A Visitor's Impression of the Wellington Rose Convention

(Written as Vice-President of the SA Rose Society; condensed from an article published in *The Australian Rose Annual* 1964, page 129.)

The spring flush of roses was all over, except for a few late flowering floribundas and some of the old fashioned roses, when I left Renmark to drive 160 miles to Adelaide to catch the plane for Sydney. I then had to spend the night there before flying to Wellington on Tuesday 12 November [1963]. It was uncomfortably hot and humid in Sydney but really cold and windy when I arrived in Wellington, and this made me understand why the spring flush of roses in New Zealand is a month later than in the warmer parts of Australia.

On entering the Wellington Town Hall I was most impressed with the beautifully decorated foyer and staircase, which contained a most tasteful blending of pink and mauve schizanthus, primula, forced hydrangeas and tall conifers in pots, with standard fuchsias and variegated abutilon for accent.

On the eve of the show there was an official welcome to delegates and the guest of honour, Mr Sam McGredy of Northern Ireland, held his audience enthralled with his amusing anecdotes. His stories were a sheer delight.

During the next day the All New Zealand Rose Show was staged. I was most impressed with the quality of the blooms flown in from each of the twenty-two district Rose Societies of New Zealand to help make the Show such an outstanding success. The first thing that staggered me as I looked at the exhibits was the size and, above all, the intensity of colour of the yellow and copper varieties. 'Goldene Sonne' was absolutely breathtaking, 'Mojave' had an intensity of colour I thought incredible and 'McGredy's Yellow' was almost the same colour as 'Spek's Yellow' is in Australia.

I thought the general staging and management of the show was really outstanding, and I would like to congratulate the Wellington Rose Society on their magnificent effort. It was estimated that 4000 people were at the official opening.

The next morning took us all – 650 enrolled for the Convention – to the Lady Norwood Rose Garden, containing 1800 bushes in beds of one variety set in lawn with a central fountain and a curved pergola on three sides and the begonia house as a backdrop. I liked the idea of floribunda roses intermingled with an occasional standard rose around the edge of the garden and the use of climbing roses interspersed with bigger Kordes shrub roses round the pergola.

I was surprised to see how low the bushes were pruned in the winter. Hybrid teas had been cut to 12 inches (30 cm) and floribundas to 6 inches (15 cm) from the ground. It was the hardest pruning I have ever seen and I think it was starting to drastically reduce the vigour of the bushes, especially the hybrid teas. Whole beds were not likely to have more than a dozen or eighteen flowers per plant. Unfortunately, the roses had been delayed by the cold windy weather and were not very far out. It was noticeable that reds are far better in Australia but yellows are much better in New Zealand's cooler climate. I was surprised to see the floribunda 'Orangeade' heavily marked with dark shadings. In Australia this variety is a pure clear orange and really magnificent. On the other hand, 'Korona' was a far better colour in New Zealand. I was impressed with the vigour of 'First Love' in Wellington and am wondering whether it is happier on *Rosa multiflora* stock than it is on our *R. indica major* stock. In South Australia 'First Love' is often affected with rose canker.

The Begonia House at the Lady Norwood Garden was magnificent. In fact it is the best glasshouse I have ever seen. I was most impressed with the size and quality of the tuberous begonias; the display of red, orange and yellow basket begonias was lovely, and so were displays of schizanthus, hydrangeas and *Gloriosa superba*, the climbing lily of the Amazon.

The Wellington Rose Society entertained us all very well indeed. We were taken to a number of lovely gardens and points of interest. The national awards were presented by Sam McGredy, who again was most amusing. He kissed all the women prize winners, but looked a trifle worried when Dr Paterson insisted on rubbing noses with him, Maori fashion!

I was disappointed that there was no time at the Convention for a lecture by Mr McGredy. I had looked forward to hearing about the new varieties in Europe and had hoped to see coloured slides of the best of them. I heard a glowing account of his lectures at Christchurch and Auckland and was very sorry I missed them by a couple of days.

We spent a very interesting evening at a floral art demonstration given by Mrs Bennett. She said that in a fortnight's visit to the east coast of Australia a few years ago, she had seen no roses at all and wondered whether we grew any! She took the wind right out of my sails. This was followed by a talk by officials of the American Rose Society on a proposal to form an International Rose Society to try and iron out differences between the rose societies of different countries and clear the way for international rose shows and conferences. The discussion that followed was profoundly interesting.

A combined church service on the Sunday morning was the grand finale of a wonderfully organised convention that inspired the 650 delegates to go home and strive for better roses.

Roses for the Summer in the Inland
(Written as Vice-President of the SA Rose Society; condensed from an article published in *The Australian Rose Annual* 1965, page 116.)

There are many roses that will stand up well to the hot dry conditions of our inland summers. In this article I intend to deal with those varieties that will produce good quality blooms in December, January, February and March providing the bushes are kept well watered, the ground is well mulched and the temperature does not get very much above the century mark. Those varieties that are indispensible in spring and autumn but not suitable for summer conditions must be omitted.

It is hardly necessary for me to say that a rose must have ample substance and plenty of petals to be a good summer variety.

Dealing with the hybrid teas first: of the reds, 'Chrysler Imperial' is outstanding. On a sturdy 6 foot (1.8 m) bush it produces its long-stemmed, fairly slow-opening flowers in abundance and its colour is far richer than at other times of the year. The new rose, 'Avon', has been really outstanding in its first year of trial. It is a much brighter red than 'Chrysler Imperial', one of its parents, but in all other respects very similar to that variety. I would not be surprised if it becomes my best red variety. 'Christian Dior' will also stand the heat well, although it reaches its peak of perfection in the autumn. The gaunt-growing 'Rouge Meilland' will not burn, but it is a little sparse with its flowers. 'Champs Elysées', though opening quickly, lasts very well on the bush and better than any variety when picked. It is the richest coloured red rose I know. Indispensible for hot conditions is 'Baccara', so popular under glass in France. Its smallish slow-opening flowers of a lovely burnt orange shade last as well on the plant as they do when picked. I do not hesitate to say that it is the best hot-weather variety that I grow.

There are some good pink roses for the inland. 'Confidence' is outstanding for form, colour, size and length of stem. On 8 foot (2 m) bushes it produces its beautiful blooms with consistent regularity and is one of the truly great roses for spring, summer or autumn. If I could have but one summer rose it would be 'Confidence'. Of the same colour, 'Michèle Meilland' will produce lovely blooms if given a little afternoon shade. 'Mascotte', so insipid in cool climates, is glorious here. Its very slow-opening blooms of soft pink flushed with lavender-pink at the edges will hold in the bud for days in the heat. It is a rose that should be known far better. 'Suzon Lotthé' is also a hot-climate rose, where the lovely blend of pink, salmon and lilac shades in each flower is far more pronounced than in cooler climates. The warm pink 'Astrée' produces a continuous supply of well-formed flowers throughout the year and is outstanding for the number of flowers produced and for the tremendous size of the plant. 'Anne Letts' is at its best in the hot weather when there is no dew to spoil its outer petals. It can be relied upon to hold its form in heatwave conditions. The rich pink 'Ballet' probably holds its form longer than any rose I know and is indispensible for the exhibitor.

Of the pink blends, 'Silver Lining' is magnificent at any time of the year. I think if I could only have one rose I would choose this variety as each flower is always well formed whatever the weather. A close rival to 'Silver Lining' in the summer is the Spanish variety 'Maria Teresa Bordas', a lovely combination of pink and soft yellow on a thornless plant – a martyr to black spot in coastal areas but superb in the inland. The new pale pinks 'Memoriam', 'Royal Highness' and 'Dresden' have all performed very well in their first year. 'Memoriam' has been superb in the hottest of weather. Its colour is a lovely soft pink shade – not the insipid off-white I have seen in cool climates –

'Michèlle Meilland'.
(Photograph courtesy Margaret Furness)

'Silver Lining'.
(Photograph courtesy Margaret Furness)

and its form is impeccable. In fact, my nine plants were still lovely after a week of century temperatures culminating in a day of 114° F (46° C). They were the only blooms in the garden showing no sign of scorch. 'Royal Highness' and 'Dresden', although first-class varieties, are not in the same class as 'Memoriam'. These three varieties fill a great need for good pale pink roses without salmon tones.

Of the whites, 'Message' is the outstanding variety as it opens far more slowly than 'Virgo' and does not blemish so easily. I like the hint of green in the centre of the flower. The newer 'White Butterfly' is a summer rose. It has amazing keeping qualities in hot weather but unfortunately easily marks with thrip damage in the spring.

'Virgo'.
(Photograph courtesy James Young)

Yellow roses which retain their colour are unfortunately very scarce, but I think we have a winner in the rich yellow 'King's Ransom', which was outstanding for colour stability and form last summer. The new 'Dorothy Peach' stood up well to last summer's heat and holds its form very well. It is very free flowering but is rather short in the stem. 'Amatsu-Otome' may well become the leading yellow variety. It has excellent form and a very satisfactory plant habit and was easily my best yellow exhibition rose this autumn in spite of being only a first-year plant. 'Lemon Elegance' has shown great promise too in the hotter months. Though not quite large enough for exhibition, it will make a lovely decorative variety. The pale yellow 'Burnaby' is my favourite rose in the garden for size and form. Unfortunately its outer petals quickly lose their substance once it is picked, and I have trouble keeping it on the show bench. The buff yellow 'Diamond Jubilee' is by far the best buff-coloured variety in the inland but it must have dew-free nights.

'Diamond Jubilee'.
(Photograph courtesy Margaret Furness)

In the gold to copper range I like 'Tanya', a lovely burnt copper colour. 'Thais', a rich gold of wonderful form, and the neglected variety 'Tonga', which holds its form very well indeed, can be magnificent in the autumn.

'Thais'.
(Photograph courtesy James Young)

I have been pleased with both 'Super Star' and 'Hawaii' in the heat. Both produce smaller flowers than in the spring and autumn, but retain their form and colour well. Both produce perfect bushes for vigour of growth.

The new 'Orchid Masterpiece' is the first mauve rose that holds well in the heat. Its colour is lovely but the bush is rather slow to repeat.

Turning to floribundas, I would say the outstanding red varieties for colour stability and long-lasting qualities are 'Lilli Marlene', closely followed by 'Evelyn Fison', 'Moulin Rouge', 'Siren' and 'Fire King'. All are first-class varieties. 'Spartan' is indispensible for the quality of flowers it produces in the summer and the new 'Orangeade' is the brightest and best of the many orange varieties. The round outline of the truss and the even spacing of the florets make this variety perfect for showing. The newer 'Orange Sensation', although a little prone to mildew in the autumn, runs 'Orangeade' a close second for the title of brightest spot in the garden.

In copper shades, 'Circus' and 'Dr Faust' retain their colour well and the most reliable yellow is the soft straw-coloured 'Golden Fleece'. The new 'Rumba' makes a superb border, but its florets are a little small to mix with other floribundas.

Of the pink shades I like the slow-opening peach pink 'Papillon Rose', the rose pink 'Rosenelfe' and the salmon 'Chic'. All are outstanding for form in the best hybrid tea tradition. For garden display the big heads produced by 'Rosenmarchen' and 'Sweet Repose' are indispensible.

'Iceberg' is the outstanding white floribunda for freedom of flower and habit of growth. It fact, I should think a bush of this variety would produce more flowers each year than any other variety.

Of the mauves, I like 'Lavender Girl' best in spite of its sprawly habit of growth, but I think the new single 'Lilac Charm' very lovely indeed.

Mention must be made of one climber, the soft pink 'Blossomtime' that produces five crops of flowers each year and has lovely form and substance under the hottest conditions.

I cannot over-emphasise the importance of keeping roses watered all through the summer. Many people advocate a summer rest with no water, but I consider this can easily lead to disaster. The plants will soon defoliate, red spider can play havoc and the bare canes of the plant can be severely scorched by the sun. A severely scorched plant will never recover.

I do not pretend that we can expect our best blooms in the summer months, but I do think that by carefully choosing our varieties, we can grow roses that we can be proud of at the hottest time of the year.

Growing and Showing Floribundas

(Written as Vice-President of the SA Rose Society; condensed from an article published in *The Australian Rose Annual* 1966, page 77.)

Since the introduction of the first floribunda roses they have become increasingly popular each year until at the present time well over one half of the rose bushes sold in the world each year are floribundas. In Europe particularly, floribundas in beds of one colour have largely replaced annuals. What a wonderful sight these masses of one variety must be!

In Australia the floribunda rose took longer to become popular, probably due to three factors. Firstly, the ease with which hybrid teas are grown in our mild climate (in cold climates floribundas are less liable to frost injury than hybrid teas); secondly, the limited numbers of parks and large gardens where floribundas could be used for massed bedding; and thirdly, I think, because of the refusal of some keen rose show exhibitors to see beauty in anything but a high-pointed exhibition hybrid tea variety.

However, more and more discerning garden enthusiasts are finding that floribunda roses provide much more colour for each unit area of ground than any other plant. Geraniums, I should think, would be their closest rivals. Floribundas will flower from early October until late June or even, if winter frosts are not too severe, until well into July. Last year 'Spring Song', 'Iceberg', 'Zambra' and 'Circus' were still quite colourful in mid July.

'Circus'.
(Photograph courtesy James Young)

Floribundas are very effective used in groups of one variety to provide a massed effect of even height. However, there is such a wealth of material to choose from that gardeners can plant either in groups of harmonising colours or contrasting colours. I have tried to group my roses in informal drifts of one colour, either slowly changing to a different colour or changing with sharp contrast from red to yellow or red to white, which can be quite spectacular.

Just as important as the general colour scheme is the grading for height. One of my rose borders has five rows of roses on each side of a central grass walk and it is here that grading is all important. I suggest that much thought should go into the ultimate heights of the varieties to be planted or much of the general effect will be lost.

Some people think that all floribundas grow to the same height, but they range from 'Pinkie', which reaches just 18 inches (45 cm), to 'Korona' and 'Diamant', which can easily reach 8 or 9 feet (3–3.5 m) in two years. As far as planting is concerned, the same rules apply as for hybrid teas except that dwarf floribundas such as 'Pinkie', 'China Doll' or 'Meteor' can be planted 24 inches (60 cm) or even less apart for massed effect, and some of the larger growers such as 'Spartan', 'Daily Sketch' or 'Red Wonder' need at least 3 feet 6 inches (1 m).

Pruning is much the same as for hybrid teas except that the bushes can, if necessary, be pruned a little harder with no ill effects. As far as manuring is concerned, I give all my roses a dressing of all the fallen leaves I can find from my many deciduous trees in late autumn, and a dressing of Nitrophoska® in August and again in early March. The early March dressing is the heavier – approximately 1 pound (450 g) to every eight plants.

Regarding the showing of floribunda roses, I think it is a pity that many very important rose shows have so few classes for floribundas, miniatures, old-fashioned and species roses. The general public sees the same exhibition varieties year after year, while at the same shows there is scarcely a class for decorative or garden varieties – and still fewer for floribundas. This, I think, is a great pity, as so many of the best garden and cutting varieties are not suited to the exhibition show bench and the ordinary home gardener orders a number of varieties seen at the shows that are quite unsuitable as garden plants.

Here at Renmark eight years ago we divided our floribunda roses into three classes: multiple heads, cuts showing up to seven blooms per head, and solitary blooms with buds allowed, classed as floribundas, hybrid tea type. I am happy to say that this classification has been adopted by the National Rose Society of South Australia. The multiple heads can, of course, be enormous – watershoots of some varieties showing up to forty, fifty or even sixty buds and flowers are not unusual. They are staged individually in tapered cones 3 inches (8 cm) in diameter at the top. These fit into a tapered hole in the show bench so that it is impossible for them to topple.

Now a good head of a floribunda is just as hard, if not harder, to find than a good exhibition rose! The outline of the head should be circular in formation, the individual blooms should not be too close together or too far apart, and they should all be equally distributed within the circular outline. All the flowers should be as fresh as possible, whether they be buds, half open or fully out. Any spent flowers can be removed from the truss as neatly as possible and any gap in the truss can sometimes be closed by wiring the flowers in the position you require them the night before the show and removing the wires before judging. Any laterals rising above the main head should be removed.

The classification for floribundas up to seven blooms in a head is for those varieties that do not have such big heads of bloom. Unopened buds are not counted but a careful watch must be kept in case more than seven blooms unfurl before judging.

The third class is always a very interesting one, as it caters for those varieties that produce exhibition-type blooms. The same variety can be shown in all three classes! We have found that this rather complicated system has worked very well indeed and has added enormously to the public interest in floribundas.

This brings me to packing floribundas for a show. Should the show be nearby, I pack them all in buckets of water with all thorns removed in case of damage to petals. However, for the Melbourne Rose Show this is not practical, as I have to travel 140 kilometres by road to Mildura and then by plane to Melbourne. I pick the heads the morning before the show, plunge them into deep water immediately and then, in a cool garage, I completely de-thorn and tidy up the trusses. For packing, each head is put into an orchid tube with a pierced rubber washer on top to take the stem. If the stem is too large to go into the test tube, a balloon is used instead. The head is then carefully wrapped in fine tissue paper and the stems are packed vertically in a very large cardboard carton so that the long stems all rest on the bottom. For a class of nine bunches, six stems to the bunch, this little job can easily take five or six hours. Of course, wiring of floribundas is out of the question. If the heads are floppy they are not worth showing.

Regarding the best varieties of floribundas to grow, there are so many excellent varieties that it is hard to make a choice. Of the reds, 'Evelyn Fison' has a wonderfully rich colour, good substance and a very compact head, and 'Lilli Marlene' is more dwarf in growth and darker in colour. 'Orange Sensation' is an outstanding orange with everything one could wish for in a floribunda – colour, form, excellent growth and freedom from disease. 'Spartan' is an excellent salmon-orange variety that I place next to 'Iceberg' for general garden display. 'Anna Wheatcroft' is an enchanting single with lovely gold stamens and an attractive soft orange colour, but it will not travel long distances without bruising. There is a charm of simplicity in single roses that is totally lacking in exhibition varieties.

'Evelyn Fison'.
(Photograph courtesy Margaret Furness)

Of the bicolours, 'Circus' is, I think, still the most reliable. There are not many good floribundas in the yellow shades. 'Allgold' and 'Gold Cup' are excellent in the garden but seldom produce a good-sized truss. However, they are the best of the bright yellow varieties. Of the whites, 'Iceberg' is, I consider, the best garden rose of all and my favourite pink is the old 'August Seebauer', a large bloom of soft rose pink with an old-fashioned cluster of petals in the centre of the bloom – it looks equally at home with modern or old-fashioned varieties. The new biscuit-coloured 'Violet Carson' has superb form and a huge head of flowers. It should perform very well on the show bench.

The lavender-mauve floribundas are all very spreading in growth. It is very hard to get them off the ground. However, all are sturdy and free flowering. I like 'Lavender Girl' for its rich colour and good form, 'Gletscher' for its soft rose-mauve shade and 'Lilac Charm' for its single blooms with golden stamens – a delightful combination.

I have left two of my favourites till last – both in a new shade of rich golden apricot. 'Zambra' has only a few petals, but its tightly scrolled buds are very beautiful and it opens to show golden stamens and lasts particularly well, both on the plant and as a cut flower. 'Woburn Abbey' has flowers of superb form and substance although not as freely produced as those of 'Zambra'. Both are superb floribundas in a particularly bright colour. It must be stated, however, that all the varieties I have mentioned as outstanding are grown in a hot dry summer climate with an abundant water supply from irrigation and no black spot. They may not behave so well in moister, cooler climates.

'Woburn Abbey'.
(Photograph courtesy James Young)

The Land of Ena Harkness: A Visit to Tasmania

(Condensed from an article published in *The Australian Rose Annual* 1967, page 102.)

Our roses in South Australia were completely finished when I visited Tasmania for the Burnie Rose Show in November 1965. I had heard so much of the quality of the exhibits at Burnie that I was expecting a great show and I was not disappointed.

In spite of a strong wind three days beforehand, the exhibits were well up to the standard I had expected. But by far the most outstanding rose of the show was 'Ena Harkness' – never have I seen such depth of red, such size or form. There were dozens of blooms of this variety and I was told that 'Ena Harkness' has been the best red at every Burnie Spring Show to date. Likewise, 'Elizabeth Arden' has always been the best white. Other outstanding roses, huge and very well formed, were the ubiquitous 'Diamond Jubilee' and 'Silver

Lining' and 'Mrs George Geary', which must have a cool climate. 'Stella' was the loveliest I have ever seen her, softest ivory-buff in the centre and rich carmine on the outer petals. 'Mrs Sam McGredy' was very large and well formed – this variety, too, likes a cool climate.

The champion bloom was a superb 'Kordes Perfecta' staged in the novice class. It had thirteen rows of spectacularly bi-coloured pink petals symmetrically arranged around a high pointed centre, wonderful texture and a circular outline, a rose certainly in its most perfect phase of its possible beauty. It was one of the best blooms I have ever seen. The runner-up also came from a novice class – a wonderful bloom of 'Isabel de Ortiz', coloured a rich pink. The novice roses were very well staged and of excellent quality. The champion bunch was a lovely arrangement of the bright pink 'Editor McFarland'.

I was pleased to see good strong heads of floribundas on display. 'Iceberg', 'Border Queen', 'Frensham' and 'Chinatown' were all outstanding. As in New Zealand, 'Orangeade' was a dull colour. It is surprising that a rose from McGredy is far better in our hot climate.

I was most surprised with an exhibit of 'Complicata', fully 5 inches (13 cm) across, showing lovely golden stamens, while 'Sparrieshoop' was so rich a pink that it was hard to believe that it was the same rose that we grow in South Australia.

I will never forget my visit to Mr Richardson's garden. There was a large number of huge watershoots on each bush, just about to break into bloom, and the last of the spring flush was finishing. It was incredible to think that in this garden there would be no gap between the first and second flushes. Mr Richardson's garden is on a very steep slope overlooking the town and the sea, and the hillside has been terraced into beds that hold two rows of plants between each stone retaining wall. The soil has been built up several feet in each bed and is ideal for growing roses. Almost all the bushes were in perfect condition – fifteen bushes of 'Ena Harkness' were a picture. I think 'Ena' has won the hearts of all the male rose growers in Tasmania, as she seems to be their favourite, and no wonder!

The new roses impressed me very much indeed – all grown in last year's nicely composted dahlia bed! Three-month-old bushes were 3 feet (1 m) high and just smothered in watershoots.

A visit to the Burnie Park Rose Garden was most rewarding. 'Climbing Sutter's Gold' and 'Climbing Editor McFarland' were a picture, which made me think that the Editor is probably still the best deep pink hybrid tea in Tasmania. 'Chinatown' was 7 feet (2 m) high and the flowers were as big as hybrid tea blooms but in great clusters. It impressed me as much as any rose I saw in Tasmania. Unfortunately, in South Australia, 'Chinatown' has a virus disease. The planting of the bright red 'Evelyn Fison' and 'Saratoga' around the War Memorial in the park was an excellent idea.

After a very enjoyable trip to Queenstown and Strahan via the famous beech forests, we set forth for Launceston. The roses here seemed a little later than those at Burnie and were right at their best. Floribunda heads were very large and I saw bushes of 'Moulin Rouge' and 'Spartan' 8 feet (2.5 m) high and 6 feet (1.8 m) wide. 'Masquerade' was just as good and a hedge of spur-pruned 'Paul's Scarlet Climber' at York Park Oval, forty-five plants in all, was really outstanding.

We called at St Finn Barr's School, whose Sister Xavier is one of the leading exhibitors at the Launceston shows, and found a wonderful collection of roses in good condition. Some of the standards growing against the wall of the church were 10 feet (3 m) high and Sister Xavier had a new area of exhibition varieties that augurs well for the future. The parks and gardens at Launceston impressed me very much, especially the new Rhododendron Trust Garden at the Punch Bowl, and of course, the lovely Cataract Gorge.

I addressed a meeting of rose enthusiasts at the home of Mr Poxon, Vice-President of the Launceston Horticultural Society, and hope that a branch of the Tasmanian Rose Society will soon be formed at Launceston.

Leaving Launceston on the way to Hobart, I was intrigued at the excellent topiary work along the Midland Highway, all due to the keen work of a highway employee. The animals and birds are really works of art and are a wonderful tourist attraction.

Our next call was to Mr Bisdee at Bagdad, and his gracious old-world garden that had an Alister Clark look. I was delighted at the blending of old and new varieties growing in happy unison. A huge old 'tree' of 'Lamarque' was growing over the house, its nodding flat quartered white blooms a joy. The noisette 'Mme Alfred Carrière' was 10 feet (3 m) high and 12 feet (3.75 m) across, and a 'tree' of 'Flying Colours' growing up a tank-stand had a trunk like a forest tree. The soil in this sheltered valley was black and extremely fertile and the hybrid tea roses were staging a comeback after a disastrous frost in

'Lamarque'.
(Photograph courtesy Margaret Furness)

October – the same frost that had decimated a lot of apple and pear crops. I had never seen roses frosted before, but the midlands had been badly hit and a lot of bushes looked as though they would not flower until Christmas. I was delighted to find a bush of 'Joanna Hill' in fine condition, a rose that should not have been allowed to disappear from our gardens in the rush to be first with the latest. I also saw an old bush of Alister Clark's 'Daydream' that is so beautifully illustrated in J. Horace McFarland's book *Roses of the World in Color.*

Continuing on to Hobart, the first thing that I noticed was the Hobart Rose Garden at the intersection of the Midland and Tasman Highways. What a perfect spot for a public rose garden! The garden was an absolute gem of imaginative design and maintained in excellent condition. The skilful blending of colour in beds that held two varieties must have been the work of a true rose lover. The floribundas definitely stole the show – solid blocks of one variety that were of even height and just laden with bloom. The standards of 'Iceberg' astounded me, and there were lovely heads of 'Lilli Marlene', 'Firecracker', 'Sarabande', 'Sweet Repose', 'Paddy McGredy' and 'Café' – 3 feet (1 m) high and with no weak necks!

There were several charming little beds of miniatures set in the lawns, highlighted by miniature standards, and a border of 'Scarlet Gem' was delightful. Last but not least was a bed of newly planted rugosas that will give a great deal of satisfaction in future years, pride of place going to 'Frau Dagmar Hastrup'. The labelling was extremely well done and the whole garden was a credit to the Tasmanian Rose Society and the Hobart City Council. It must be one of the most photographed spots in Hobart.

The dynamic Tasmanian Secretary, Mrs Knight, showed me around some lovely local rose gardens and took me to Mt Wellington where there was still a little snow. Hobart impressed me as one of the loveliest cities in Australia. I must also comment on the wonderful work and enthusiasm of the Tasmanian Rose Society in planting and pruning so many rose gardens at hospitals, homes for the aged and schools.

I flew home from Hobart with unforgettable memories of Tasmania's friendly people, good rose-growing climate, lovely countryside and superb roses. I will return to the land of 'Ena Harkness' as soon as possible to enjoy these delights once again.

Roses for Floral Arrangements

(Condensed from an article published in *The Australian Rose Annual* 1970, page 62.)

It is most important that roses be thoroughly conditioned before they are used for arrangements. I cannot over-emphasise the importance of picking either very early in the morning or at dusk and placing the blooms immediately into water as you pick. This is imperative if you want your roses to keep. I remove the bottom three or four leaves as I pick, but do not remove the thorns until the blooms are taken inside. I like to leave the blooms up to their necks in cool water for at least six hours before arranging. This helps them to last better, especially if they can be put in a refrigerator. The period of cold seems to delay the opening of the buds and they do not blow so quickly.

A number of you probably carry roses long distances to shows. I find that they carry much better in a car if they are wrapped in rolls of wet newspaper than carried in buckets. If they are packed into solid cardboard boxes they stay cool, as wet paper is a good insulator and the darkness also delays opening. The two major elements causing roses to open are, of course, temperature and light, so the cooler and darker the blooms are, the better. Nothing makes a rose go limp more quickly than putting it in a hot car. For short distances roses will carry in buckets. Pack the buckets with cypress foliage then shear it off at the top. Push the stems in and they will not move about. It is far more effective than wire netting and far easier to remove the blooms on arrival.

Rose buds are easy to pack as they can be bunched tightly together but, naturally, choice exhibition-type blooms for focal areas in massed work and for modern work must be treated with great care. They are safest if packed on bolsters in cartons where the blooms do not touch each other. After all, if you have gone to all the trouble to grow good roses it is important that you get them to the show in first-class condition. Incidentally, if the weather is very hot, it is wise to put your rose-stems in scalding water for a few minutes after picking. This does add to their life and if you have carried blooms in boxes out of water for six or more hours, it is a good idea to re-cut the stems and again put them in scalding water for a few minutes as soon as you unpack them. It is most important that sappy watershoots be put in boiling water, also very young foliage.

In arranging roses so many people seem to look for gladioli for a background as soon as they have a massed arrangement to do. I am the reverse. I like gladioli for moderns, but I much prefer light foliage, blossom or dried material for a background to a massed arrangement. I think gladioli are too heavy to use at the top of any arrangement.

To use all roses you must have long stems, the longer the better, and this is not always easy. Some cultivars will never produce long stems however well you feed them, but fortunately there are some in each colour that can be chosen which have 3 or 4 feet (1–1.5 m) of stem, given good growing conditions.

In a massed rose arrangement the buds must be long and slender to give you that 'spiked' flower effect to contrast with the rounded forms of the flowers in your focal area. There are a number of cultivars that have lovely elegant long buds and these are the ones we need. First and foremost is 'Eiffel Tower' – a rich pink bud of the utmost elegance on very tall slender 4 foot (1.5 m) stems. It is a seedling of 'First Love' and no other rose in my garden is used as much for picking. Then there is 'Queen Elizabeth', whose stems are so thick they can take up all the room in your urn before you have the focal point in at all, but what a lovely colour she is. Then in pale pink I like 'Royal Highness', a soft colour of great appeal on a superb bush and finally the new 'Columbus Queen', a two-toned pink on a very floriferous bush. 'Columbus Queen' is probably my first choice as a garden cultivar.

Turning to red, we have 'Christian Dior', the stems of which are very long, 'Mr Lincoln', which has a lovely rich colour and glorious foliage, and in dark red there is 'Papa Meilland'. In orange-red we have 'Baccara', the longest lasting rose I know, with that lovely dark shading to the outer petals that many a judge has penalised as a blemish. Another orange-red rose with amazing length of stem is 'Allegro', not well known but a must for massed arrangements. There is also 'Montezuma', but in my opinion the new 'Bel Ange' is an improved version of 'Montezuma' as it has wonderful stems and is pinker.

'Buccaneer' and 'Goldrausch' ('Golden Giant') are both deep yellow with very long stems. These two always have a bend to the stem just below the bud, which makes them ideal for a flowing asymmetrical massed arrangement, but you will be in trouble if you try to do a highly stylised symmetrical triangle with them. In buff yellow there is 'Fred Howard' on 4 foot (1.5 m) stems. He tones in beautifully with 'Vienna Charm', 'Diamond Jubilee', 'Apricot Nectar' and 'Champagne', giving a very rich subtle buff to gold colour scheme. In gold we have 'Vienna Charm' and 'Valencia' whose colours are

'Christian Dior'
(Photograph courtesy James Young)

'Papa Meilland'.
(Photograph courtesy James Young)

so stunning and which go so beautifully with dried material, and in white there is 'Mt Shasta' with buds of good length and interestingly tinged with green, 'Pascali', which should be in every garden for its freedom of flowering, and 'Virgo', which I consider the ultimate in refinement in a rose bud. And last of the long-stemmed beauties is the new 'Carla', a bud of great elegance in the most beautiful shade of soft salmon-pink. These then are some of the best cultivars for background work for massed arrangements of roses.

We now turn to those roses with sufficient fullness to be suitable for focal areas in massed work and for bold moderns. Stem length is not important here. In the deep pinks there are 'Eden Rose', 'Ballet', 'June Park' and 'Maria Callas'. All have ample petals and they are all lovely when at the full-bloom stage. We do not see enough full-bloom roses in massed arrangements. Big rose arrangements need some full roses to give that transition from bud to full bloom. Exhibitors are scared that the judge will say 'past their prime' – I say that a rose at the full-bloom stage with the stamens still fresh is one of the most beautiful of all flowers.

'Memoriam' and 'Anne Letts' are pale pink and 'Mascotte' is a lovely soft lilac. Then there is 'Silver Lining', a two-toned pink of wonderful substance, and lastly the shimmering coral pink 'South Seas', quite stunning at full bloom and wonderful for bold modern work. 'Mme A. Meilland' needs no boosting from me, as nothing can be lovelier, while 'Chicago Peace' in rich pink and yellow should soon be equally popular.

In glowing orange we have 'Super Star', the orange and biscuit coloured 'Queen of the Roses', which lasts for ten days when picked and opens very slowly, and the lovely ruffled 'Hawaii', all good for modern arrangements where impact of colour is so important.

In gold there are various cultivars – 'Vienna Charm', 'Thais', 'Beauté' and 'Valencia' – all are musts for moderns. There is my favourite in richest chrome yellow, 'Dr A.J. Verhage', which has such lovely form and stunning colour, and is wonderful arranged with glycerined copper beech. In bright yellow, 'Summer Sunshine' is by far the best cultivar. In white, 'Message' is probably the strongest contender and, in mauve, 'Eminence' is simply glorious in rich red-violet with wonderful substance. In red we have the incomparable 'Christian Dior', 'Avon', 'Chrysler Imperial', 'Black Velvet' and 'Red Devil'.

Floribundas are not seen enough in massed or modern

arrangements. There are some wonderful colours and some of the heads of seven or so florets can be lovely in modern work. The truss can be treated as one big flower in modern arrangements. The floribundas are very handy as fillers between the elegant buds of the outline and the strong round flowers of the focal area. They give graduation in size and often can tone beautifully with their hybrid tea sisters. In dark red there is 'Europeana' with its lovely plum-coloured foliage, while the scarlet 'Evelyn Fison' and orange-red 'Moulin Rouge' and 'Fidélio' are pleasing to the eye. There is 'John Church' of orange-red 'Super Star' colouring, 'Woburn Abbey' is good in gold and also the lovely single 'Zambra', 'Orangeade' – surely the best floribunda of all for eye-catching moderns – and the slightly deeper 'Orange Sensation', all of which should be used more than they are at present. Then there is the red and yellow 'Charleston' – so cheerful – and the soft colouring of 'Apricot Nectar' which tones so well with 'Diamond Jubilee'. Turning to the soft colours in the biscuit and peach shades, 'Violet Carson' has lovely form, as has the peach and gold 'Sonora'. These are just a few of the floribundas which can be used effectively in floral arrangements.

For that special arrangement we have some lovely old species roses with wonderful foliage. There is *Rosa sericea pteracantha*, grown for its large red translucent thorns that are so fascinating in the spring and for its soft ferny foliage. Also *R. rubrifolia*, whose foliage is a lovely subdued grey-plum colour, which looks enchanting with red-violet roses and is so handy when doing a monochromatic arrangement in red-violet. Incidentally, if the schedule says 'monochromatic red-violet', for example, then the foliage has to come off the roses and *R. rubrifolia* foliage can be substituted, but when the schedule states an arrangement of flowers 'in tints, tones and shades of red-violet', then I consider the green foliage should stay on. I hate to see roses stripped of their glorious foliage. They look so naked. There are *R. hugonis* and its relatives, all with ferny foliage of great refinement, and *R. fedtschenkoana* with foliage of a lovely soft grey. We have the roses grown for hips and these too are not used nearly enough. *Rosa moyesii* and *R. moyesii* 'Geranium' produce hips shaped like flagons, of a fiery orange colour, that are perfect for use with the floribunda 'Orangeade'. The rugosa roses of such distinctive foliage have hips like large strawberries and are eye-catching when used with holly foliage at Christmas time. Then there are *R. woodsii fendleri*, whose

Rosa rubrifolia.
(Photograph courtesy James Young)

hips match 'Christian Dior' and which last on the bush all the winter, and the large maroon hips of *R. pomifera duplex.* Combined with roses in massed arrangements these hips can be lovely.

Miniature roses are becoming increasingly popular. They are ideal for posies and miniature baskets and can give that touch of lightness to bouquets. They can be lovely too when used with candlesticks. There are many cultivars available but a few are really outstanding – 'Rosmarin' in soft pink with a reddish centre, 'June Time' in clear pink, 'Baby Darling' in apricot, 'Scarlet Gem' in rich red, 'Cricri' in salmon-orange and the new yellow 'Gold Coin' are my favourites.

There are a great many more roses that can be used effectively in floral arrangements but I suggest that if you grow these cultivars they will give you a good foundation of the types of blooms suitable for floral arrangements. May you enjoy developing your artistic flair in your leisure time with roses.

My Favourite Rose
(Condensed from an article published in *The Australian Rose Annual* 1970, page 146.)

'Iceberg' used in a winter arrangement.

What a request! I have thought about it for several days and dearly want to say 'Dr A.J. Verhage' because gold is my favourite colour, but then I have some misgivings. Will I get enough blooms from it! Does it repeat quickly? Is it disease free? Does it open slowly in the summer and yet stand up to winter cold? Can I pick it, and pick it, and still have a good bush?

After all these thoughts I have discarded 'Dr A.J. Verhage' in favour of the floribunda 'Iceberg'. My reasons are: an enormous bush; at least twice as many flowers each year as any other cultivar; no disease troubles at all – rare in a white rose (we have no black spot in this part of the world, but I have heard a rumour that this cultivar black spots in more humid climates); the ability to flower all the time from shoots that come from behind the flower heads; the lovely shape of the buds; and the neat form of the open flowers. Petals drop cleanly when the bloom is spent and I marvel at the amazing way in which this rose will flower through June and July unspoiled by rain or heavy frost and will hold on to all its foliage until, in desperation, I prune it in late August. Surely 'Iceberg' must be my favourite.

A Floral Arranger's Favourites
(Contribution to a symposium; published in *The Australian Rose Annual* 1972, page 130.)

I have given my list of six favourite roses much consideration and list them in order of preference:

'Eiffel Tower' My number one cut flower rose. It has good length of stems which are pliable with few thorns and is a prodigious bloomer.

'Mr Lincoln' A good rich red colour with good blooms throughout the season, an important consideration which makes this one of my best red cultivars.

'Avon' Another red which has often been overlooked. I am always short of red roses for arrangements and this one, a better grower than 'Chrysler Imperial', is included in my list for its fragrance and excellent foliage instead of 'Christian Dior' and 'Super Star'.

'Dr A.J. Verhage' My favourite rose colour is yellow so this one is my next nomination as it grows superbly in my area. The rich yellow blooms are a lovely colour and the flowers when fully opened with their amber stamens are a joy. Each year I plant more bushes and this is a test of a good rose in my garden.

'Thais' Although this cultivar suffers from black spot in some less favoured climates, this disease is almost unknown in my climate. The apricot buds flushed red are a mainstay when doing colour schemes in apricot to gold.

The last place has taken me weeks of deliberation and I have finally chosen **'Peter Frankenfeld'** for its superb form, its slow opening and its beauty in all stages from bud to full bloom.

'Eiffel Tower'.
(Photograph courtesy Margaret Furness)

A huge bowl of 'Mr Lincoln'.

A figurine in cast iron contains an autumnal mass of 'Gold Medal', 'Thais' and 'Dr A.J. Verhage' roses.

Thoughts of a Roving Exhibitor
(Condensed from an article published in *The Australian Rose Annual* 1972, page 83.)

I have exhibited roses and arrangements of roses in most of the states of Australia and have scrutinised a number of overseas shows and their schedules. My conclusion is that while there is little difference in our ideas of a good exhibition rose, our standards of judging decorative roses, floribundas and arrangements of roses vary considerably.

We are in agreement about 'what is the most perfect phase of a rose's possible beauty' for an exhibition rose but our methods of exhibiting them are very different. The Royal National Rose Society (England) and the Rose Society of South Australia exhibit roses in boxes covered with moss – only 2 inches (5 cm) of stem is visible with an added leaf or two on the moss. The effect is attractive when it is done well and it does allow an exhibitor to use short-stemmed cultivars which could not be used if staging in tubes. Quite often these roses are clipped onto a wire and it is impossible for a judge to observe the back of each rose (which is sometimes a great help to the exhibitor). The Rose Societies of Victoria and Tasmania apparently look at these exhibition boxes with scorn and their rules stipulate that roses must be staged in the tubes provided by the Society; they allow wiring and extra foliage may be added. Sometimes the bad placement of this foliage too high under the flower looks unnatural and occasionally an exhibitor uses it to support an outer petal about to droop down, hoping the judge will not see it.

The other Australian states and the National Rose Society of New Zealand stage roses with longer stems, no wiring or added foliage, and the New Zealand rules provide that 30 points of a possible 100 are awarded for stem, balance and foliage. I think that exhibition roses should be staged in this manner, with good stems, no wire and their own foliage.

Garden roses as distinct from exhibition roses are a feature of the shows organised by the Rose Society of South Australia and this class caters for all those cultivars which are too small or have too few petals to be of exhibition standard. I refer to those grand cultivars such as 'Eiffel Tower', 'First Love', 'Virgo', 'Michèle Meilland', 'Beauté', 'Bettina', 'Charlotte Armstrong' and 'Lotte Günthart'.

Garden roses are staged with long stems and side buds must be retained. They are picked from the garden – no disbudding, no pelleting – and are judged at the half-open stage. In New Zealand they are referred to as decorative roses and are a feature of shows in that country.

Rose societies must be urged to sponsor garden roses at their shows, as at least three-quarters of the good roses grown today are in this class. Why then are they seen so seldom in some of our major shows in Australia? Judges have developed an exhibition bias, unfortunately, and a period of education may be necessary. When this class of rose is judged, exhibits which contain exhibition-type blooms such as 'Diamond Jubilee', 'Silver Lining', 'Chicago Peace' and 'Christian Dior' should be down-pointed. They are too full-bodied for this class.

The Rose Society of New South Wales includes a class for decorative roses – cultivars like 'Queen Elizabeth', 'Whisky', 'Audie Murphy' and

'Golden Shower' – that show their stamens when at full bloom. They must have fewer petals than exhibition or garden types and they are judged with preference being given to multiple heads. Some blooms should be at full bloom, some should be in bud, others in various stages of opening. They are staged three stems (not blooms) to a vase and make up a fine display.

The judging of single roses is uniform at all shows that include this class (many do not) – they must have five petals and be circular in outline. 'Nancy Hayward', 'Dainty Bess', 'Golden Wings', 'Fervid' and 'Altissimo' are reliable cultivars for the single rose class.

There are many differences in the floribunda classes. Ten years ago the Renmark Garden Club attempted to sort these roses into three classes:

• Hybrid tea type, one bloom on each head, unopened buds allowed.
• Up to seven blooms on each head.
• Multiple heads.

This system has worked well and was adopted by the South Australian Rose Society and those in Victoria and Tasmania. I think these divisions have sorted out the floribunda dilemma quite well. In my meanderings around the shows, I have seen some shocking decisions, however, with one champion award given to a truss that was twice as long as it was wide. A circular outline and an even spacing of blooms and buds within this outline are all important when judging this interesting class.

The Rose Society of New South Wales usually has a magnificent display of floribundas at their major shows. They are displayed in vases with a stipulation that there should be no more than twenty-five florets to each vase. They do not stipulate a maximum number of stems, with the consequent result that the keen exhibitors have discarded all their cluster floribundas and are growing 'Pink Parfait', 'Redgold', 'Violet Carson', 'Evelyn Fison' and the like – which produce mainly single buds. The result is that the winning bunch is usually a magnificent floral art display of twenty-five stems of such roses as 'Redgold' or 'Pink Parfait'. Anyone with any skill at arranging a bunch of roses must realise that it is infinitely easier to arrange twenty-five single stems in a vase that perhaps five stems with five flowers on each – and, of course, the effect from the front is superior.

The New Zealand Rose Society has a good system for judging floribundas. They have decorative stems which must have fewer than four florets on each stem, and others which must have more than four.

To quote from their judging rules, 'the spacing and arrangement of flowers and buds, balance and shape shall be taken into consideration but not the type of flower'. To me this seems to be an excellent system.

Miniatures are becoming increasingly popular at shows now and by far the best display I have seen was at the New South Wales State Championship at Nambucca Heads in April 1971. They were staged three cuts to a little vase and the individual shape of each truss could then be easily judged.

Classes for the old treasures, the old-fashioned types, are usually included in most show schedules and at the spring shows in South Australia. I have seen up to twelve entries for the section asking for three distinct cultivars. Some exhibitors are pruning these old albas, damasks, gallicas and centifolias fairly hard, resulting in huge blooms with the characteristic flat, quartered appearance, which has created much interest among the general public.

These are the features I am looking for more and more at the rose shows which I attend – a display that shows the Queen of Flowers in all her infinite variety. To have a hall crammed full with glorious full-bodied exhibition blooms is not good enough. We must have, if possible, a happy mixture of exhibition blooms, garden types, floribundas, miniatures and old-fashioned cultivars, staged singly and in bunches. May I suggest that to make our shows more comprehensive to include all types of roses, show organisers should adopt the policy of the New Zealand and New South Wales rose societies and award the medal and amateur championship – the highest award in the show – to a class of three exhibition roses, three garden roses and three floribunda roses. Surely the champion exhibitor could then justly claim to be the best exhibitor of roses, in the three main types, at the show. The display for the public would then show the rose in all her infinite variety.

My Twelve Best Floribunda Roses
(Contribution to a symposium; published in *The Australian Rose Annual* 1980, page 100.)

Your request for my favourite twelve floribundas puts me in trouble immediately – whether to choose hybrid tea types with only four or five flowers to the head, or large-headed types. I have compromised and decided to list six of each.

Multiple Heads

'Europeana' A marvellous rose with lush red-tinted foliage and huge heads of long-lasting flowers of lustrous dark red with a velvety sheen. Good exhibition type.

'Rusticana' The bright vermilion-salmon blooms open from red-tinted buds. It produces flowers from ground level which makes it a suitable rose for a hedge. It is a good keeper and marvellous producer.

'Bobby Dazzler' Its colour is a soft salmon-peach and the form of the individual blooms, produced on long stems, is sheer perfection, with huge round trusses of plump buds opening into long-lasting lustrous flowers.

'Caid' This rose produces big heads of evenly spaced blooms of a vibrant orange-flame colour with good red-tinted foliage. Its growth is moderate and compact and the flowers have excellent lasting qualities on the bush and when they are cut.

'Daily Sketch' An unusual plum and silver bicolour rose with attractive foliage, strong sturdy growth, trouble free, and well-spaced heads that always attract attention.

'Apricot Gem' I predict this rose will be planted in many gardens for its sheer loveliness of colour, excellent shaped heads of good size and long lasting qualities. A rose with impact and good for the show bench.

Hybrid Tea-type Floribundas

'Prominent' A very tall upright bush with good red-tinted foliage, long-stemmed flowers with many petals of an intense red-orange, and very fragrant. They have splendid form with lasting qualities. This rose is ideal for the flower arranger.

'Prominent'.
(Photograph courtesy James Young)

'Friesia' I find this bright yellow floribunda has intense colour with no fading and a perfection of form from tightest bud to full bloom. The bush is moderately vigorous.

'Bengali' This is a small rose on 18 inch (45 cm) stems. The tight bud is very long and pointed, making it ideal for posies. The rich apricot-gold colour is very appealing and the bushes are free flowering with very vigorous growth.

'Gypsy Moth' I first discovered this rose in New Zealand in 1971 and it has been a great favourite of mine ever since for its exquisitely formed, deep salmon-coloured flowers of enormous size. Colour stability is excellent. The bush is healthy of medium height. There are very few thorns.

'Apricot Nectar'.
(Photograph courtesy Margaret Furness)

'White Spray'.
(Photograph courtesy James Young)

'Apricot Nectar' A very tall spreading bush producing vast quantities of very soft apricot-buff flowers of superb form. The colour deepens in late autumn and early winter. It is excellent for picking; if disbudded, the flowers on long stems look like large hybrid tea roses.

'White Spray' From the late Edward Le Grice, this rose is a mighty grower, about 8 to 9 feet (2.5–3 m) with healthy foliage, long stems and clusters of beautifully formed creamy white flowers of great substance. A lovely rose to act as a foil for the multitudes of flamboyant varieties.

Early Spring–flowering Roses
(First published in *The Australian Rose Annual* 1984, page 35.)

In the warmer areas of Australia, there are some roses which will reach their zenith of beauty in the month of September and thus join the crab-apples, pyrus, forsythias, lilacs and wisteria in bringing spring colour to our gardens before the hybrid teas and floribundas come into flower in October.

My first climber to flower is always *Rosa* x *fortuneana*, discovered by Robert Fortune in 1840 in a Chinese garden and considered to be a hybrid between *R. laevigata* and *R. banksiae alba-plena*. This certainly looks plausible, as both parent species can be seen in its flowers and habit of growth. *Rosa* x *fortuneana* usually starts to bloom in late August and reaches its peak in late September, when my plant, covering a large implement shed and cascading down from the top, over an area of 30 feet by 30 feet (9 m by 9 m), is a sight to behold. It is quite evergreen and the very full, quartered cream flowers, about 2 inches (5 cm) across, come on short stems all along the great cascading canes. Scent is quite pronounced and this is a wonderful climber to grow into trees, over buildings or on strong fences.

Next to come into flower and reaching its peak in late September is *Rosa laevigata*, a species again indigenous to China. This species has become naturalised in the southern states of America, where it is known as the Cherokee rose. To me, this is the queen of all climbing roses. The plant habit is superb, with great climbing shoots clothed in 'spring' green foliage, producing single pure white flowers with wavy petals and gold stamens all along the branches on 4 inch (10 cm) stems. Some of the canes can be 8 to 12 feet (3–4 m) long and the effect in full flower is a sight to remember. I have this rose cascading down from the top of a shed, where its full potential is realised. I also have one budded to a tall standard, where it weeps down to ground level and is in full flower a month or so before any other weeping rose.

Flowering a little later than *Rosa laevigata* is the hybrid 'Anemone' and its sport 'Ramona'. 'Anemone' is a cross between *R. laevigata* and a tea rose, which accounts for the later flowering. They reach their peak in the first fortnight of October and I find the deep carmine single flowers of 'Ramona' most attractive. Both are strong growers, but not quite as rampant as *R. laevigata*, nor are their flowers as beautifully formed.

Again from China and in full bloom in late September are the banksia roses – and what a sight they are. The double yellow must be one of our choicest climbing plants, with the advantage of no thorns and evergreen foliage. Introduced into England in 1824, it has not proved hardy in cold climates, but in Australia it is a fitting memorial to Sir Joseph Banks. The double white banksia, *Rosa banksiae alba-plena*, is probably even more vigorous than the yellow form. The clusters of small flowers are most attractive and it has the added advantage of a very strong perfume of violets that scents the air for a considerable distance. Not so well known is *R. banksiae normalis.* My plant is young, but the single white flowers are very pretty in a simple kind of way and the perfume is very strong. There is also a single yellow form, *R. banksiae lutescens*, which I have not seen.

The last of the early spring-flowering climbers is *Rosa gigantea*, which is living up to its name. I planted it at the foot of a 50-year-old Lombardy poplar and it has reached 30 feet (9 m) in a few years. It is now climbing over a tree nearby. As I write this in early October, the whole poplar tree is festooned with single deep cream flowers and the ground underneath is carpeted with petals. *Rosa gigantea* is for large country gardens only; it must have room to develop.

Lastly I will mention the Alister Clark climber 'Flying Colours'. This flowers earlier for me than the better-known 'Nancy Hayward'. 'Flying Colours' is a single, very rich cherry pink rose of great vigour. I find that the more it is pruned, the more it grows, so I have finally tamed it into a huge great ball about 12 feet high and 20 feet across (4 m x 6 m). All I do each year is to give it a haircut by reducing all the shoots that stick out too far. In early October the effect from a distance is of a great big bowl of roses.

Now let us turn to a few early spring-flowering shrub roses, all of which are yellow. My favourite is 'Golden Chersonese', produced from a cross between *Rosa ecae* and 'Canary Bird' by a former President of the Royal National Rose Society, Mr Ted Allen. This rose seems to have inherited all the good points from both its parents. It gets its wonderfully rich yellow colour and its upright growth from *R. ecae* and its small flower size from the paler yellow 'Canary Bird'. It grows upright to a height of over 7 feet (2 m) and the canes are covered from top to bottom with a multitude of ¾ inch (2 cm) single flowers, set among ferny foliage. From a distance it can be mistaken for a forsythia. It reaches its zenith in late September, as do both its parents.

Times of flowering will be later in colder climates. If your hybrid teas do not flower until November, then these roses mentioned will flower in October. These roses all add so much variety in size and shape and form to our rose gardens apart from their early spring flowering.

Where is Australia's Biggest Rose Bush?
(First published in *The Australian Rose Annual* 1984, page 114.)

In England, we are told, at Kiftsgate Court in Gloucestershire the remarkable specimen of *Rosa filipes* 'Kiftsgate' covers an area 50 feet by 30 feet (15 m by 9 m) and grows up through an enormous beech tree. I saw this rose in full flower last July and it was a remarkable sight, which will remain in my memory forever.

In America we hear of a double white banksia at Tombstone, Arizona, under which 150 people can dine at once, and this too must be an unforgettable sight. It takes the honours for the biggest rose in America!

What do we have to offer in Australia?

To start the ball rolling, I can boast of two large specimens. One is of *Rosa* x *fortuneana* which climbs up over an implement shed and then cascades down from the roof. I removed the sides of the shed to show off the beauty of the rose that has grown over an area of roof 30 feet by 30 feet (9 m by 9 m) plus all over a rainwater tank at one side of the shed near which it is planted. As I write this in late September, the bush is covered with what must be a million very double white flowers and it is a marvellous sight. The plant is about thirty years old.

My other offering is *Rosa gigantea*, which is planted at the foot of a

80 foot (24 m) Lombardy poplar behind our garage. It has clambered 30 feet (9 m) up the tree and half of it has hooked itself into a *Robinia pseudo-acacia* near at hand. The whole tree is festooned with large single cream flowers and the robinia is flowering at the same time with its racemes of cream pea flowers shaded brown at the centre. The whole effect is lovely. The rose is about twenty years old.

I wonder what other big climbing roses there are in Australia or New Zealand. I am sure there are a lot scattered around old houses in most of our states and many of them, I should think, would have interesting histories.

A Tale of Five Mermaids
(First published in *The Australian Rose Annual* 1984, page 137.)

Many years ago I ordered two 'Mermaid' roses from a Melbourne nursery. They arrived as poor plants – about 2 inches (5 cm) of stick and that was all. I planted them and for the first year growth was yellow and sickly and I thought they would never flourish. However, after that, off they went. They made gigantic thorny canes several metres long in all directions, and kept smothering 'Mrs George Geary', 'McGredy's Yellow' and 'Sutter's Gold' planted nearby. They then started climbing up through a young prunus and an apple tree. Because they were quite unmanageable I decided on drastic action: I would remove them with a tractor and chain. This was done and I thought all was well. Unfortunately they were both on their own roots and shot up from severed roots in all directions – they soon became just as large as they were before. So I left them and they are still there, growing slightly subdued under the shade of lots of trees and still flowering well.

One of the offshoots from these 'Mermaid' roses has been planted near a large work shed, where it has gone right over the top of the roof of the shed and up into a large golden ash tree. It is a glorious sight in late spring when most other roses have finished flowering. The only pruning that is done occurs when the huge canes cascading down from the roof get in the way of passers-by.

But the greatest 'Mermaid' of them all is one on a post and wire fence along the roadside that I planted with 120 climbing roses in 1957. Most of these roses are hybrid teas and floribundas, but one section at the end contains an enormous tangle of climbing 'Lorraine

Lee', 'Wedding Day', white and yellow banksia roses, 'Nancy Hayward' and 'Mermaid'. This section blew down in a storm in 1970. The only thing to do was to cut all the climbers down to nearly ground level with a chainsaw, carry away the tangled remains with the tractor, put up a new fence and start again. This all happened in early December. All the climbers came away again except 'Mermaid', who reacted strongly to such drastic treatment and died! However, there was a little layered piece 10 feet (3 m) from the parent plant which I kept and it prospered. Now, fifteen years later it has completely smothered 'Anemone', 'Climbing Dainty Bess', 'Meg' and 'Danse du Feu', and is cascading down from a large prunus tree. The display of blossom is a wonderful sight, enormous heads of flowers all summer and autumn.

My last 'Mermaid' I have really tamed. I budded her onto a weeping stock and she makes a lovely big standard, but grabs any unsuspecting passer-by with those vicious fish-hook thorns.

Well, that is the tale of my five 'Mermaids' and I really think five is enough for anyone.

As a final comment, when I visited the Royal Horticultural Society's marvellous garden at Wisley in 1968 and again in 1976, I was delighted to see 'Mermaid' behaving admirably on a warm chimney on the charming old office building. No rampageous growth here, but subdued and controlled, really beautiful in flower. I went back last July to a very sorry sight. Poor 'Mermaid' had been smitten by the disastrously cold winter of 1981–82. She had been killed right down

'Mermaid'.
(Photograph courtesy family of James Young)

to the ground, leaving a 4 inch (10 cm) diameter butt, from which one sickly shoot had managed to grow, covered with mildew. It had grown from the back of the stump right against the warm chimney. It will be years, if ever, before she regains her former beauty. 'Mermaid' is certainly more at home in our warmer climate. I advise anyone who wants a really good bush of 'Mermaid' to grow her on her own roots and put her out in the middle of a paddock!

A Day with Peter Beales

(Condensed from an article published in *Heritage Roses in Australia*, Vol. 9, No. 2, May 1987, page 9.)

Peter Beales was a welcome visitor to Australia when he came in October 1986 as a guest speaker at the World Heritage Rose Conference that took place in Adelaide. We left the conference in the delivery van which had brought down all the conference decorations, and meandered in a leisurely fashion through Birdwood and Mt Pleasant, stopping where necessary to allow him to photograph massed displays of Salvation Jane (*Echium plantagineum*) among the rocky outcrops. This weed is used as a bedding plant in England. In a garden in Birdwood we spotted a huge and magnificent unpruned bush of 'Sutter's Gold' and a hedge of *Rosa indica major* with petals looking quite translucent in the late rays of the sun. We proceeded on to Walker's Flat, where the old cliffs took on an ochre-red colour in the light of the setting sun. All was reflected in the still waters of the Murray River – an unforgettable sight.

At Swan Reach Peter took the helm of the van. He couldn't believe it when he drove 58 miles (92 km) to Loxton, dipping the lights only once – a real taste of outback Australia! We took over six hours to get home instead of the usual three, but I think it was worth it.

As we drove past my roadside plantings I pointed out 'Mermaid' growing up a huge prunus tree, the yellow and white banksia roses as well as the old climbing hybrid tea roses planted in 1956. Further on, Peter was also impressed with two huge bushes of 'Lamarque', a lovely bush of 'Fortune's Double Yellow', and the gigantic *Rosa* x *fortuneana* growing over the tractor shed. These varieties are all tender in Norfolk. As we pulled up at the house, he said it was worth coming just to see that first glimpse.

Banksia roses sprawling in all their glory in Coleen and David Houston's garden at Hay in New South Wales.

Next morning dawned clear and hot with century heat forecast, our first really hot day for the season. Decked out in my smallest pair of shorts and a bush hat, and laden with camera gear, Peter was ready for the day. And what a day it was. We went around all the old roses first where my first query was a huge mound of the early rambler, 'Aglaia', pure white flowers in an elongated truss and once flowering – definitely not correctly named. Peter had never seen it before, so it is still a mystery. I had always been suspicious of a bush of 'Reine des Centfeuilles', which Peter identified at a glance as 'Seven Sisters' (*Rosa multiflora platyphylla*). I showed him my two bushes of what I had known as 'Seven Sisters' – which were of a variety he had never seen before.

Then it was on to the beautiful old tea known as 'Octavus Weld', as it grows on that gentleman's grave (1911) at Blakiston cemetery; it has been propagated by many of us. It is a most variable rose. In the spring it is large, flat and very double in a buff-apricot tone. Peter called it 'Safrano'! Now, William Paul's portrait of 'Safrano' is very double, but most later authors call it 'semi-double-loose'. Were there two varieties with the same name? But to continue with our Octavus. In the second and third flushes, the hot weather changes him to a peachy pink colour, a similar shade to 'Jean Ducher' [now correctly named 'G. Nabonnand'] and he loses a number of petals. Then in June and July he flowers magnificently, gaining even more petals than in the spring and turning the colour of clotted cream. A quite remarkable rose.

As the day became hotter the roses began to flag. I was forced to turn on the irrigation. I will always remember with affection the sight of Peter taking photographs and wearing my knee-high rubber boots. I managed to get a photo of him lying on his back by the pond taking a shot of a white *R. multiflora* seedling; a procumbent Peter Beales, complete with shorts and a bush hat!

Late in the afternoon I put Peter on the bus for the long trip to Sydney. He kept awake all night hoping, unsuccessfully, to spot a kangaroo and described the 20-hour trip as very interesting if not tedious. My cup of joy overflowed when he wrote in my copy of *Classic Roses*, 'My feet are wet but I've just had one of the best days of my life'.

Thank you, Peter, for coming to Australia and joining in all our Conference activities and for writing *Classic Roses*, which will be our rose bible for many years to come.

Diamond Jubilee Celebrations of the Rose Society of Western Australia

(Condensed from an article published in *The Australian Rose Annual* 1993, page 77.)

In October 1992 I spent a very happy five days in Western Australia as a guest of the Heritage Rose group and the Rose Society of WA, to attend the Diamond Jubilee celebrations of the Rose Society. I was met at the airport and taken to see the Heritage Rose convenor, Noelene Drage, and her lovely garden of roses and companion plants, before attending an enjoyable informal dinner at the Rose & Crown Hotel at Guildford. A huge bush of 'Bloomfield Abundance' (now known as 'Spray Cecile Brunner') at the inn was reputedly the oldest rose in Western Australia, so the innkeeper said, planted in 1840. This was a bit far-fetched as 'Cecile Brunner' was not bred until 1880 and 'Bloomfield Abundance' was introduced in 1910! The bush must have been planted soon after that.

It was then on to joint convenor, Carol Mansfield, at Carmel and her English garden looking lovely with lots of nicotiana, foxgloves, hellebores and camellias snuggling nicely in a secluded valley.

The next day we had a barbecue luncheon at Araluen, now an official botanic garden for the Hills area. Hundreds of white tulips were putting on a great show, but the roses were only just showing colour. The present magnificent, large rose garden of both old and new roses growing with a backdrop of native bush was in the planning stages when we were there.

Mary Hargreaves from Kalamunda gave us a buffet meal and we walked around her garden where roses vie with huge camellias, wonderful magnolias, taxodiums, conifers and all kinds of cool climate plants – a real plant lover's garden with an amazing collection of water iris, daylilies and shade-loving plants.

A highlight of my visit was a trip down to Pinjarra to see the old rose garden created by Colonel Frost. There were a lot of teas and noisettes out and I was able to sort out a few unknown roses, but several baffled me. Forty people attended from as far afield as Albany, and they brought me lovely foxgloves, cornflowers, poppies, sweet peas and other goodies to use with Pinjarra old roses for a flower demonstration in some old containers I'd brought over with me. The Pinjarra garden, completely run by volunteers, is well worth a visit for anyone visiting the West.

I was then handed over to the Rose Society of WA. My genial host, John Coleman-Doscas, had a foot in both camps. I was the guest of the tireless secretary, Connie Ryan, for the rest of my stay. Connie's roses, like my own when I left home, were all buds but looking very promising.

The WA Rose Society Spring Show was smaller than usual, the same as the Adelaide and Melbourne shows, because of the cold, wet spring, but it was of excellent quality.

On the last day John Coleman-Doscas had promised me a quick tour of Perth's antique shops before my departure, but we soon found that they were all closed on Mondays, so we paid a visit to the superb formal garden of Peter and Tania Young. Tania (nee Verstak) is a former Miss World and just as charming as I expected. Their garden, formal in design, but softened by plants tumbling over walls and archways, was one of the most enchanting gardens I'd seen in Australia, with most effective use of subtropical trees, combined with cool climate plants.

But all good things must come to an end and it was off to the airport to return home to prepare for the Renmark Show.

The Judging of Old-fashioned Roses
(Condensed from an article published in *The Australian Rose Annual* 1994, page 70.)

One of the most difficult classes in rose and general shows is the judging of the Old Rose classes. No one wants the job. This even occurred at Hampton Court in England for the great Summer Show last year when I was given the job.

What is an old-fashioned rose? Personally, I think an old rose, like an antique, should be a hundred years old. Some schedules preclude all hybrid teas and floribundas, which are classed as moderns. How can you judge 'La France' against 'Admiral Rodney'? Surely 'La France' is an old rose.

How about all the roses prior to 'Peace'? They could be put in a 'nostalgia' class – 'Ophelia', 'Crimson Glory', 'Talisman', 'President Herbert Hoover' and 'Texas Centennial' should make a good section at a major rose show.

The hybrid musks could be classed as shrub roses along with all the Kordes shrub roses – 'Berlin', 'Bonn', 'Sparrieshoop', et cetera.

I think with the hundreds of thousands of David Austin roses grown in Australia, all schedules should have a section for these. Should this class include roses such as 'Pierre de Ronsard' and 'Cardinal Hume'? Other breeders, particularly Meilland, are producing Austin-like roses. Their trial ground at Lyon contained a lot in soft apricot and peach shades.

I'm not so concerned about Rose Society shows. There is usually a class for most roses. But what about general shows? Recently I judged at Mildura Show and a class for a bowl of old-fashioned roses contained a bowl of 'Reine Victoria', one of 'Sparrieshoop', another of 'Pierre de Ronsard' and one of 'Heritage'. Only 'Reine Victoria' was really correct, but the flowers were stale and thrip marked. If the schedule had stated 'old-fashioned type roses', all would have been eligible.

With the enormous interest in old roses all over the world nowadays, classes for old roses and old-fashioned type roses would be a nice foil to all the classes for hybrid teas, floribundas, and bunch classes. Surely a nice bunch of 'Heritage', 'Abraham Darby' or 'Swan' is as attractive as one of 'Diamond Jubilee' or 'Red Queen'.

In Praise of 'Marie Leonida'

(First published in *Journal of Heritage Roses in Australia Inc.*, Vol. 18, No. 1, Autumn 1996, page 18.)

A bowl of 'Marie Leonida' showing the deep segmentation of the blooms.

(Photograph courtesy James Manifold)

In 1957 I planted two long fences of roses along the roadside to protect the garden inside from the dust from the gravel road. The road has been sealed for many years, but the roses have remained. Among these is 'Marie Leonida', growing next to that vigorous old once-bloomer 'Silver Moon'. For years 'Silver Moon' grew rampantly and nearly smothered her, but now 'Marie Leonida' has taken on new vigour and is holding her own and has even escaped up a large poplar tree.

As I write this in a February heatwave, 'Marie Leonida' is doing us proud, smothering herself in a huge second crop of very double cream flowers on thorny *R. bracteata*-like growth. Never have I seen such a quartered flower. Each segment is divided right into the centre of each flower to make four quarters and this is most attractive. I always thought 'Marie Leonida' was a cross between 'Mermaid' and a yellow tea rose, but on looking up the American Rose Society publication *Modern Roses 5*, I find that 'Marie Leonida' is said to be a cross between *Rosa bracteata* and *R. laevigata*; it's curious that the most double rose I have ever seen should turn out to be a cross between two singles.

Anyway, whoever her parents are, why is 'Marie Leonida' such a forgotten beauty? She flowers from November until June, her *R. bracteata*-like foliage very beautiful. She has never had a trace of mildew or black spot although she does suffer from thrip discoloration in the spring, as does every other pale variety. She is quite evergreen and has never been pruned except for cutting back wanton growth. Why is she not popular? Together with 'Mermaid' and *R. bracteata*, 'Marie Leonida' never stops flowering from spring to autumn. No other climbing roses are so free flowering.

I have never set eyes on 'Marie Leonida' in Europe – probably suffers from winter cold – but why is she not gracing all our large country gardens in sunny Australia? Hardly a rose nursery has heard of her, and she is mentioned very rarely in old rose books. She made her debut, according to *Modern Roses*, in 1832; this means that 'Mermaid' (1916) could not be a parent and neither could 'Safrano', the first yellowish tea, which arrived in 1839; the really yellow teas were developed much later. Thus 'Marie Leonida' is a most mysterious maiden.

Postscript HelpMeFind lists the parentage as 'Bengale à odeur de thé' × *Rosa bracteata* J.C.Wendl, and adds the note: 'Reportedly raised from open pollinated seed of "Thé bengale ordinaire" that was planted close to *Rosa bracteata* and thus not truly a species cross. For different speculations on parentage, see References.'

Hollyhocks and Roses
(First published in *Journal of Heritage Roses Australia Inc.*, Vol. 23, No. 3, Spring 2001, page 5.)

Many of us would love to live in a thatched cottage in the Cotswolds with hollyhocks, Canterbury bells, sweet williams, cottage pinks and, of course, old roses clambering up the walls – a far cry from home at Renmark on a hot summer's day with a north wind and a plague of thrip!

However, one thing I can grow in abundance among the roses is hollyhocks. They are nearly becoming feral. There is a slight ridge under the roses, which are furrow-irrigated, and the hollyhocks seem to revel in a dryish area around their bases and a moist root run. I grow singles and doubles – the doubles are very beautiful but their flowering period is shorter. As I write this on July 1 there are still quite a few clumps in flower. When I pick hollyhocks for an arrangement I place the stems in near-boiling water and they last up to seven weeks. The buds open all the way up the stems and individual flowers stay open for two weeks.

When in France I saw a gorgeous strain with very deeply divided leaves, and flowers in shades of salmon and apricot, at Odile Masquelier's garden at Lyon. I begged her to save me some seed after she had cut them down. When she came to Australia for the Heritage Rose conference in Western Australia she brought me lots of seed, but nearly all flowered in shades of pink.

Here hollyhocks start blooming in late October, reaching their peak in late November – some spikes reaching 13 feet (4 m). I cut them back to the ground after Christmas and they come again in autumn and early winter. Many people will not grow them because of rust. Here rust does not do much damage and I am told by an expert from the CSIRO that hollyhock rust is a different type from rose rust.

The great advantage of growing them is that they flower between the first and second flush of roses and, with daylilies and shasta daisies, help to give colour at a time when there is not too much in flower after the deluge of colour in October. I find they do best when seed is just scattered on the ground where required.

A forest of hollyhocks in my garden.
(Photograph courtesy Margaret Furness)

Viru and Girija Viraraghavan, India

(Condensed from an article published in *Journal of Heritage Roses Australia Inc.*, Vol. 23, No. 2, Winter 2001, page 25.)

Viru and Girija Viraraghavan live in a small town called Kodaikanal, perched high in the mountains behind the steamy city of Madras, at an altitude of 7000 feet (2150 m). Winters are cold with some frosts and summers are very wet at the onset of the monsoon rains.

Viru is a retired civil servant – he retired early to pursue his interest in rose breeding. Girija has been editor of the *Indian Rose Annual* for the past fifteen years and is an expert on rose products and rose history. Viru believes very strongly that we need evergreen roses for hot climates, roses that will stand summer heat and even partial flooding, and roses that will flower all the year. He is using *Rosa gigantea*, *R. bracteata*, *R. wichurana*, *R. sempervirens*, *R. laevigata*, *R. banksiae* and above all *R. clinophylla*, a species that will stand flooding for three months per year in the delta of the Ganges and yet also be found growing in desert country. All these species are evergreen and form large mounds, and by crossing them with some of the modern roses that do well in India, and using 'Bonica', a floribunda with a lot of *R. wichurana* blood, he hopes to breed some worthwhile new cultivars. Viru is using the yellow form of *R. gigantea* found in wet areas of Assam with promising results. He is very interested in seeing the hybrids of *R. gigantea* bred by Alister Clark, which are not grown in India.

What a transformation would take place in our Australian gardens if all our roses were evergreen – no more bare canes in the winter months! Also, all these evergreen species get next to no disease! Let us hope that evergreen roses may be the roses of this new millennium.

Chapter 8

Flowers in the Home

I have lived in the same house all my life. My father built the first section in 1922 and additions were made later. Three rooms – the drawing room, dining room and the summer sitting room – have jarrah panelling which gives a very warm look and is a great background for old furniture. Reproductions of the Old Masters are hung on the pale apricot upper walls. The wooden picture frames tie in well with the panelling, while many of the mounts have a narrow band of blue between picture and frame which complements the blue in the pictures and the blue ornaments in the rooms.

When flowers are in very short supply in winter or when summer is very hot I often use artificial flowers in my antique containers – peonies, fritillarias, tulips, delphiniums and iris – along with dried yarrow, globe artichokes and statice.

A three-tiered stand holds yellow roses, camellias, berries and small pompon chrysanthemums. Red roses at the centre tie in with the red candles at the top.

I am very fond of David Austin roses as they flower most of the year and can be used in period arrangements when old roses are not available. Here the cast-iron urn is packed with the soft apricots and yellows of 'Symphony', 'Charles Austin', 'Abraham Darby' and 'Troilus'.

In late winter an alabaster bowl holds almond blossom, lovely *Magnolia soulangeana* and eriostemon sprays. The long silken catkins of *Garrya elliptica* make an elegant focal point. The rose print by Redouté probably features *R. gallica* 'Violacea', *R. alba* 'Maxima' and *R. centifolia*.

An ornate vase contains a simple arrangement of almond blossom with pale pink camellias. Redouté prints act as a background above the sideboard and continue that touch of blue.

Another arrangement on the sideboard contains jasmine trails, pink daisies, dwarf plum (*Prunus sinensis*), and sprays of 'Ramona', a five-petalled rose of rich cerise with a silvery pink reverse – a sport of 'Anemone' and one of the earliest roses to bloom in spring.

This sideboard arrangement holds mixed roses combined with blue salvia, myrtle berries, hypoestes and ivy.

An unusual container of spelter with leaves and opium poppy buds holds a flowing design of lovely poppies – arranged many years ago when we could import packets of seed of *Papaver peoniflora* but not *Peonia somniferum*. They were the same!

In a black urn a merry mixture of winter flowers make a cheery statement. 'Abraham Darby' and other Austin roses, chrysanthemums, winter gladioli, South African Natal cherry, pokers, twice-blooming iris, day lilies and citrus all pick up the colours of the Flemish print.

This arrangement was made in a simple basket and placed on a table. Yellow 'Summer Sunshine' roses, white spuria iris and yellow bearded iris combine with branches of loquats. Loquat leaves have great texture and last for weeks. They often slowly turn yellow which can add to the effect.

There are many occasions where table arrangements are required. Dining table centrepieces can be conventional or very modern depending on the decor. For parties, all rooms can be decorated. Sitting rooms, halls, sunrooms, bedrooms, bathrooms and family rooms can all be enhanced by flowers. Dull corners can be brightened up with appropriate arrangements.

In the dining room, an ornate set of scales holds glass dishes filled with oasis containing 'Minnie Pearl' roses. The scales look equally attractive filled with strawberries and grapes, even dried fruit and nuts.

A silver bowl filled with tea roses whose arching stems look wonderful cascading over the table cloth. The varieties used here are red 'General Gallieni', 'Rosette Delizy', 'Homere' and 'Mrs B.R. Cant' – perfect in a Victorian period home.

A brick of oasis at the top of the stand is securely wired to holes in the top lip of the bowl to support the cascading flowers that hide the bowl – important when guests are seated. A large wreath base filled with oasis holds the lower arrangement. Mixed roses are combined with silver eucalypt leaves, amaranthus and purple grapes.

To celebrate the first roses of the year in late September, a simple bowl of *Rosa laevigata* showing its glorious golden stamens, furry sepals and rich green new foliage. This is my favourite single rose.

A silver art nouveau épergne holds the last of the David Austin 'Winchester Cathedral' rose in seven flutes at different levels. This épergne is useful for bits and pieces when flowers are in short supply and can be used for flowers such as camellias and blossom. Single roses also look very attractive in such a container.

A low oval table arrangement of 'Red Intuition' roses which are red striped with coppery pink – a subtle but stunning combination. They open very slowly and will last fourteen days when picked in cool weather. A few myrtle berries and rose hips add to the effect.

'General Gallieni' is an amazing rose. On a large spreading bush the flowers open palest pink, change through every shade of pink and end up darkest red with a mass of twisted, confused petals in the centre. Here they are placed in a copper container which I found in Japan, a real talking point for a dinner table. It is hard to believe that these roses all came from the one bush.

A simple bowl of 'Lady Hillingdon' – a rose bred in 1910. The slightly drooping stems are ideal for a bowl and perfect for cascading out of an épergne. The climbing form of 'Lady Hillingdon' is one of our most remontant climbers.

Because of their pointed buds opening to full rounded flowers, roses are interesting at all stages of development. So are tulips, iris and lilies. Some other flowers – like sunflowers, ranunculus, nerines and clivias – look best when fully opened. Roses, peonies and tulips also have good foliage to set the flowers off well. Here in a copper container a simple flowing design of the salmon-pink rose 'Arianna' looks at its best when used alone.

'Julia's Rose', named after Julia Clements in 1976, is here mixed with 'Honey Dijon' (2003) in an old copper chafing dish. The centre of 'Honey Dijon' has a much better form than 'Julia's Rose', both in the bud and full bloom. It also keeps much better. The dish was brought to Australia in 1838 by my great-grandfather, the Rev. Ridgeway Newland.

Three fluted glass containers hold a collection of old tea roses including 'Etoile de Lyon', 'Homere', 'Mrs Herbert Stevens', 'Lady Hillingdon' and 'Maman Cochet'. This would make a good centrepiece for a Victorian or Edwardian home. Some people dislike stems showing but I think it looks very natural. The flutes hold the roses in place.

Chapter 9

Rustic Arrangements in Country Gardens

I like country gardens that are a bit wild – usually because we take on more than we can manage. Also, we get slower as we get older! One advantage of the wilder garden is that we can find interesting things like loops of wisteria growing up trees, ivy clinging to poplar bark, twisted kiwi fruit vine and palm spathes of many types, all of which can be added to flower arrangements. Asparagus vine is useful too, as well as huge branches of elm with its soft chartreuse flowers.

There are five months of blossom to use, from *Prunus mume* in June, to early ornamental peaches as well as flowering plums, apples, quinces and mulberry.

The fig tree with its grey winter outline and immature fruits comes in very handy, as does the medlar with attractive brown fruit. I often use the large yellow fruit of the quince and my favourite, the pomegranate, as well as persimmons and citrus in abundance. Grapes picked with long branches look much more natural than bunches of grapes wired onto sticks.

The thorny *Poncirus trifoliata*, which comes in many forms, is the rootstock of many citrus. One of its forms is the incomparable 'Flying Dragon', whose angular branches and lethal thorns look spectacular when added to arrangements. 'Flying Dragon' is unusual among citrus in that it is deciduous in the winter, which shows up the bare thorny tracery of the tree.

I have had two large rustic wooden tables made, one from crepe myrtle (*Lagerstroemia*), and the other from yew, the makings for both coming from my garden. Thinking it had died, I once cut down a huge old crepe myrtle, whose lovely zigzag growth and mottled bark is ideal to use in rustic arrangements. The large off-cuts were used for one of the large tables. The smaller branches were made into several low tables to house low woven containers filled with succulents, grey driftwood and flowers. To my amazement, the stump of the crepe myrtle burst into flourishing growth the next spring. The other large table was made from a rather scruffy-looking yew. I had been told that the only conifer that would shoot again after being cut hard was yew. Mine, however, died after the operation.

Having lived in the same house and garden for eighty years I now realise that you spend half your life trying to gain protection for your plants and the second half removing the surplus and dealing with fallen trees. As the garden ages you get more and more of fewer and fewer varieties.

In my Garden 2005

A small table made of crepe myrtle wood holds a low container crammed full with autumn goodies from the garden. Groups of yellow sunflowers and their seed heads combine with African marigolds and the additional yellow of large rose hips. The red pomegranates are softened by the use of silver gum leaves, wormwood and *Stachys byzantina* (lambs' ears). Variegated privet and clusters of gum nuts complete the picture. I placed this arrangement at the side of a meandering path leading to an outdoor red gum setting protected from the weather by a grove of black bamboo. A huge poplar tree gives summer shade. Such displays can last over a month in cool weather.

A large basket of mixed flowers of hollyhocks, hypoestes, Japanese anemones, salvia, eucalyptus and 'Simply Magic' roses on a rustic table made of crepe myrtle wood under a huge oleander.

This green metal pot plant stand in a corner of the garden holds a large bowl of hollyhocks, perennial asters, Japanese anemones, pale pink 'Royal Highness' roses, 'Queen Elizabeth' roses and the silver foliage of *Eucalyptus pulverulenta*.

A crepe myrtle bench again, with a parallel design of 'Vienna Charm' roses, delphiniums, yellow spuria iris, cut blood oranges, cut lemons, green echeveria, cornflowers and ornamental corn in two boat-shaped woven containers.

A small table of crepe myrtle wood with yellow pokers (*Kniphofia ensifolia*), sunflowers, *Banksia prionotes* and browning aspidistra leaves in a dip-tin which used to be used in the drying of sultanas in the Riverland. Many kniphofias flower in late April and are very useful for autumnal designs.

An old basket containing a spike of yucca, and variegated ivy with 'Tineke' roses mixed with white dahlias. A very simple arrangement but quite effective. To emphasise the cream colours in the flowers and foliage, the basket is placed on an artistic swirl of cream taffeta.

(*Right*) At an outdoor luncheon for a rose group, the table arrangements were based on 'Ellen Terry stands' in which flowers are placed low on the table and then in a high bowl rising from the centrepiece. Conversations take place between the two layers of flowers. These stands are now very popular on round tables for weddings and look very dramatic. Roses used here were 'Vienna Charm', 'Pierre B' (an apricot sport of 'Dr A.J. Verhage'), 'Adolph Horstmann' and 'Thais', lightly mixed with white perennial aster. Ellen Terry was a famous Shakespearean actress in the late Victorian and Edwardian periods. She loved arrangements of simple flowers, especially sweet peas and roses.

'In a Country Garden' 2008

These four arrangements were done in the Port Lincoln garden of Vicki Rice as part of a demonstration entitled 'In a Country Garden'. I placed arrangements throughout the garden beforehand and did more in situ as the audience looked on.

An old clothes trolley filled with tall stems of entwined wisteria, kniphofia, rose hips, apricot 'Thais' roses and goldenrod

A basket on an old oven top with quinces, variegated canna, yellow roses, sunflowers and naturally twisted *Cocos plumosa* palm spathes matching the colour of the oven.

Here fruit, vegetables and flowers are arranged in an old milk can which has been placed on a rustic bench in front of a huge white jasmine bush. The yucca at the top matches the pumpkin and butternuts at the base with blue salvia, perennial asters, seed pods of *Magnolia grandiflora*, rose hips, quinces on branches and 'Copper Gem' roses.

A large old milk urn with its lid as an accessory adorns a pathway. In drought conditions the yucca excels and flowers twice a year. Here it is mixed with variegated privet, white 'Pascali' and red 'Christian Dior' roses – a good way to brighten up a dull corner.

Camawald: 'Farm Implements' 2009

One of the most enjoyable demonstrations I have done was with the help of talented arranger Danny Hoffmann at a gala weekend at Sue and John Zwar's garden, Camawald, at Coonawarra in the south-east of South Australia, a region famous for its red wine. The garden covers 4 hectares and merges from lush green lawns and exotic trees with herbaceous plants near the house to native trees and drought-hardy plants like succulents, salvias and acanthus growing under majestic red gums, some of which are several hundred years old. John Zwar has amassed a large assortment of old farm implements and these were used in the display we did, totalling forty creations in all.

Collaborating on an arrangement with Danny Hoffmann.

An old wagon wheel with grape vine loops holds a simple rustic arrangement of yellow sunflowers and yellow spuria iris grouped in two placements. The brown centres and seed heads of the sunflowers tie in with the colour of the wheel. This was a very quick arrangement.

Placed among silver stachys, two tin containers of different sizes hold dramatic loops of *Asparagus horridus* and thalictrum, beautiful purple-blue spuria iris, and artichokes to give weight to the focal area. The roses are the highly perfumed 'Fragrant Plum' and 'Chartreuse de Parme'.

A trug basket containing groups of flowers as though just picked from the garden. On the right are soft brown spuria iris, purple statice and deep blue iris, pink everlasting daisies and a grouping of 'Silver Lining' roses. On the left, blue iris and deep brown and purple iris are used with touches of blue salvia. It looks colourful at the base of a rough-barked crab-apple.

Fascinating old loops of wisteria have been fastened onto an old rusty cultivator. A cast-iron cooking pot holds a mass of 'Bonica' and 'Iceberg' roses combined with watsonias, pale blue iris and silver artemisia. The arrangement, made by Danny Hoffman, has been placed on an old tree stump for extra height.

A beautiful moon-shaped basket made of wire holds a plastic trough sprayed a rusty colour. It holds brown spuria iris in several shades with a centrepiece of 'Copper Gem' roses. It is placed on a driveway of shredded eucalyptus bark and looks very natural in a native plant section of Sue's garden.

An old weighing machine has been placed against a silver birch trunk with a cast-iron water fountain used as the container in which I arranged an assortment of white foxgloves, white alstroemeria, creamy green succulents, achillea and 'Moonstone' roses.

An implement wheel holds a blue and orange combination of kniphofias and 'Just Joey' roses at the base, mixed with blue spuria iris, statice and 'Thais' and 'Monica' roses – one of my favourites for picking as it looks great at all stages of development. The mulch makes a good unobtrusive background.

Danny Hoffman put together a pavé design on the tray of the 1923 Dodge and surrounded it with old red gum wood, which makes it particularly attractive. A similar floral arrangement to that at the front of the vehicle was made in the tray. A pavé design is a low arrangement using groups of flowers, fruits, foliage, wood and succulents of contrasting forms and textures. It is often used on low tables and viewed from above.

John Zwar's 1923 Dodge buckboard was placed under a huge golden elm with arrangements to tie in with its rust-coloured body. Here a cast-iron pot holds weathered old red gum wood and grouped 'Sophy's Rose', green euphorbia, blue iris, salvias and delphiniums, yellow roses and silver succulents.

In the back of a 1978 Holden ute a parallel design in two long woven baskets ties in well with the cover of the ute. Salmon-pink kniphofia, a chance seedling in my garden, faintly pink *Gladiolus colvillei*, and a spire of strong salmon-pink gladiolus are used for verticals. The Meilland rose 'Arianna' is mixed with euphorbia and groupings of artichoke.

An old butter churn with its lid as an accessory holds an interesting combination of airy dianella, mixed mauve-pink roses 'Lagerfeld', 'Shocking Blue' and 'Fragrant Plum', penstemon, sweet william and a head of ornamental kale. A grouping of globe artichokes ties in with the colour of the churn.

Seasonal Arrangements in my Garden

A classic fibreglass urn painted bronze-olive, with red hot pokers, oak and autumnal liquidambar leaves, 'Mercedes' roses and red amaranthus tassels with a background of a liquidambar at the end of the long rose and perennial border in my garden, which was planted in 1957. The roses are still vigorous at 52 years and are part of our major collection of pre-1960 hybrid teas and floribundas. I put their longevity down to light pruning – reducing the plant each year to no less than two-thirds of its height.

At Christmas time a huge stone-coloured fibreglass urn was filled with lovely twisted stems of crepe myrtle limbs sawn from the four trees surrounding it. (One of these is visible on the left.) Agapanthus stems were cut short and placed in the urn to tie in with those in the foreground. The long-flowering white oleander and the old house that can be seen in the background date back to 1922.

A bird bath holds a very early spring arrangement of pure white flowering peach with a base of drought-hardy yellow-green euphorbia – a plant that self-sows and provides a source of this most popular colour. The milky white sap of all euphorbias can irritate the eyes, and care is needed when handling them. Euphorbias have a dormant period before flowering and flowering increases when trimmed each year.

A rustic basket containing succulents, large shells, coral and a twisted piece of weathered wood, placed on a low wooden table to add interest in a country garden. Such an arrangement will last for months. The succulents will take root in the oasis and can be planted out in the garden when this happens.

Two large boat-shaped baskets hold a winter arrangement in the parallel style. The upper placements are red-flowering peach, almond blossom, spikes of succulent flowers and pink nerines. Grouped late roses – pale 'Memoriam' and deeper pink 'La France' – camellias and anemones are offset with bronze aeonium. Such arrangements can be done only when we do not have heavy winter frost. Minimum temperatures in the Renmark area occasionally get down to –6° C,

A butter churn with its lid leaning against the base holds a mixture of weeping golden cypress, yellow kniphofia, 'Thais' roses, apricot dahlias and bronze castor oil plant in my garden in late autumn. Part of the commercial plantation is in the background. The foliage of the castor oil plant needs to be mature for it to keep in flower arrangements. I treat it as an annual, pulling up the old plants each year.

At The Barn Palais 2010

In a large woven trug the Delbard climbing rose 'Naheema', which is sweetly scented and repeats well, is used with the silvery foliage of *Adenanthos sericea* and placed on the lawn as if just picked from the garden.

Autumn garden material – pepper-tree berries, red fountain grass, sedums that have turned a rusty red, alstroemeria and 'Eiffel Tower' and 'Lady X' roses – fill an old rustic urn which is placed on a wine barrel to give height. Behind can be seen the huge plane trees lining the driveway into The Barn Palais, an extensive convention centre near Mount Gambier, South Australia, where I demonstrated when the garden was opened as part of Australia's Open Garden Scheme.

Chapter 10

Garden Sculptures

Fifteen years ago I started to make sculptures of all sorts of interesting material mainly gleaned from my 80-year-old garden. This was to brighten up parts of the garden when flowers were scarce in heat-wave conditions in summer and during severe frosts in winter, which fortunately we don't have very often. These structures will last for several years and for special occasions the old flowers and dried material can be replaced with fresh ones.

Containers must be rustic to match the setting. Suitable vessels can include old woven baskets, discarded drums, milk urns, old separators from dairies and old ploughshares, which can be spraypainted to the required colour. Dried material might include proteas, banksias and globe artichokes – which are beautiful when picked as they show purple in the centre. I lay them on a bench in an airy shed for the stems to dry and become stiff.

For the sculptural look huge loops of wisteria are useful. Fresh *Asparagus horridus* with its sharp, very decorative thorns is very pliable and stiffens as it dries. I use fasciated material from ash trees, sunflowers and the giant white echium that looks like a cobra. Palm spathes can turn into fantastic shapes and the contrast between the smooth interiors and the corrugated exteriors as well as the difference in colour between front and back – soft beige to rich brown – is fascinating. Driftwood and weathered wood is easily obtainable along our rivers and coastlines and even white ant-eaten wood can be dramatic. We bleach our old wood to get a silvery grey look. It takes several immersions. In grape-growing areas unpruned vines with the tendrils left on are very useful. When travelling about our countryside we soon develop a seeing eye.

A simple long-lasting arrangement of green echeveria with tall stems of jade plant. The two green containers are linked with loops of defoliated green ivy. This is an arrangement perfect for summer heatwave conditions. Note the smaller matching upturned container on the left to raise the height. These are fun to do using dried material and adding fresh flowers when needed.

The fibreglass urn on a plinth holds curvaceous yacca stems with palm foliage and heads of a winter-flowering giant aloe from South Africa. It is held together by oasis covered with wire netting and tied to holes drilled near the top of the urn. Fresh flowers can be replaced after a month or so.

Throughout southern Australia xanthorrhoeas, or yaccas, are common on sandy soils. After many years they make a short trunk from which gigantic spikes emerge, packed with insignificant individual flowers which combine to make a striking cream mass. Most grow vertically, but some bend in an intriguing manner. In this arrangement the dead flowers are placed in an old drum which has been spray-painted black and then given a touch of rust. The lovely *Banksia praemorsa* is used at the base. It lasts for three months and then turns a dusky red-brown which still looks attractive. The drum is occasionally filled with water until the contents are dried.

A large urn decorated with rams' heads stands on a stone plinth. It holds a block of dry florist foam which is filled with long branches of dead silver birch limbs to which are attached five spheres of barbed wire hanging from fine wires. Unfortunately, a star-dropper post has had to be used for stability in storms. The background is an 80-year-old poplar tree, one of many surrounding my home. Such sculptures can add a lot of interest to a country garden, especially in the winter months.

On a large red gum bench stands one of two very large terracotta pots weathered to a subdued hue. It holds contorted limbs of fasciated ash tree that I noticed one night on a country road and sawed off with the aid of a torch. I've used them countless times since. Dried globe artichokes cascading downwards give weight at the base. I placed the artichokes in the arrangement just before they were mature. They then flowered to reveal striking purple centres and finally dried, showing their brown seeds. They are very attractive when viewed side on. They last about two years in a sheltered spot like this one, in front of the bamboo grove I call my 'bambooselem', an intriguing word I came across in Scotland and at Ninfa in Italy.

In Australia we have many different varieties of eucalypt bark from which to choose. In this design it is used with 'Summer Sunshine' roses, sunflowers, oak foliage and yellow kniphofias all placed in an old basket. As eucalypt bark goes limp when placed in water it is best to wire the base with skewers of hardwood.

The *Cocos plumosa* palm is very popular in hot-climate gardens. The spathes are usually straight but some bend into curves and make wonderful sculptures. The contrast in colour between the rough-textured back and the inside is very dramatic. Here they are used in an old copper placed on a wooden burl. Red-brown aeonium cuttings are placed in the oasis-packed container where they will soon make roots and continue to grow for many years. Their round form contrasts well with the vertical thrust of the spathes.

The previous arrangement after two years. The darkened colour is still attractive.

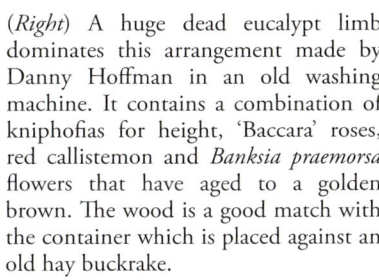

Another old blackened copper filled with oasis and making a good heavy base for the twisted spathes of *Cocos plumosa*. This time I have used a base of yellow-green *Banksia praemorsa*.

(*Right*) A huge dead eucalypt limb dominates this arrangement made by Danny Hoffman in an old washing machine. It contains a combination of kniphofias for height, 'Baccara' roses, red callistemon and *Banksia praemorsa* flowers that have aged to a golden brown. The wood is a good match with the container which is placed against an old hay buckrake.

Three small benches act as a base for a sculpture using twisted *Cocos plumosa* spathes with a centrepiece of dried globe artichokes tying in well with the design. The wall of bamboo behind adds to the effect. This has lasted for three years in the garden. I think it has a slight resemblance to the Sydney Opera House!

I acquired an ornamental tricycle and decided to get a friend to make a cyclist out of the parasitic dodder vine indigenous to our Mallee country. She took the tricycle home to get the proportions right, with one foot on the ground and the other on a pedal. Two containers painted rusty brown hold an assortment of spring flowers – anemones, roses, eucalypts, watsonia and green euphorbia. Any small flowers could be used, and autumn fruits and berries would be equally good.

For a special event we prepared groups of roses, floating on rafts of bamboo, in a pond at the base of a large fountain. Pictured here is the waterlily-like David Austin rose, 'Troilus'. Waterlily leaves add to the effect. Fine fishing line tied to a stone at the bottom of the pond anchors the rafts in place. Wire mesh was used to hold the blooms and foam prevented the creation from gradually sinking to the bottom. This looks very effective for a party in a garden.

(*Left*) The rustic table holds an old basket containing loops of wisteria combined with the bright pink David Austin rose, 'Sir Edward Elgar'. This gives colour to a shady area of the garden.

A classic urn contains oasis which supports grey succulents, sedums, purple 'Chartreuse de Parme' and 'Shocking Blue' roses with amaranthus dangling downwards. When the roses collapse more succulents can be added. A major feature is the weathered tamarisk wood which, incidentally, was taken from a large specimen which forms part of the background. Arrangements such as these do much to brighten up dull areas in a shady garden.

Chapter 11

Flowers, Fruit and Vegetables

I think that we could use fruit and vegetables in our flower arrangements far more often. There are so many forms and textures available – and the added advantage that they can be eaten once the function is over!

A samovar holds grapes, quinces, medlars and rose hips, showing how effective home-grown fruit can be.

A pair of terracotta pots placed against my garage door as decoration for a party. The fasciated wood is used with grouped strelitzia, leucospermum, sunflowers, dried ornamental corn, branches of loquats and oranges. Blood oranges are particularly effective when sliced in half. The citrus fruits are placed on skewers. If you want to use the citrus for cooking or eating afterwards, leave the skewers in the fruit as this prevents attack by the ferment fly.

A very old round table supports a 150-year-old rusty tin trunk, brought out to Port Lincoln by an early settler. A container within holds quinces, pokers, pyracantha berries and 'Gold Medal' and 'Magma' roses.

I filled a replica of an antique urn with oasis into which I placed pomegranates on curving stems to flow downwards, quinces, grapes, apples, mixed citrus and pyracantha berries, all picked from the garden.

Here a hollow stump of a poplar tree hides a 10-litre bucket which houses pieces of poplar bark, grouped kniphofias, sunflowers, branches of pineapples, quinces and three globe artichokes in different stages of development.

The old stalwart rustic table with a background of white ant-eaten poplar wood shown up against bamboo. The arrangement contains cotoneaster berries, quinces, Granny Smith apples, pumpkins, purple and green grapes, pyracantha berries, pomegranates, blue-black myrtle berries, dried sweet corn and rose hips, all picked from the garden.

I set up this display, called 'Harvest Festival', in the Renmark Institute on a bench of Irish yew with a cornucopia made by Danny Hoffmann from the aerial roots of philodendron. It contains a variety of local fruit and vegetables.

A brown and beige container placed on a red gum table with a background of bamboo holds grouped grapes, mandarins, lettuce leaves, carrots, pears, kiwi fruit, apples and capsicums. Height is obtained with a couple of heads of celery. Arrangements of fruit and vegetables have the great advantage that they last a long time.

Nothing is sacred to the flower arranger. Here an old horse-collar stuffed with damp oasis is home to grapes, apples, peaches, rose hips and succulents, with the top softened with clusters of cotoneaster berries. Mauve 'Angel Face', hot pink 'Peter Frankenfeld' and soft pink 'First Love' roses are arranged in groups.

Two boat-shaped baskets are perfect for three parallel placements of *Cocos plumosa* spathes interspersed with yellow spuria iris. The base contains ornamental grass, sunflowers, lemons – some of which are cut in halves – 'Graham Thomas' roses, an artichoke, kiwi fruit, avocados and ornamental corn and apples, all from the garden.

(Photograph courtesy James Manifold)

Two large baskets of woven material hold an assortment of spring flowers and fruits. Yellow spuria iris, sunflowers and roses are grouped with apples, avocados, green euphorbia and asparagus fern. The lower basket is turned to show its texture and to give depth to the whole. The modern pedestals don't detract from the arrangement.

The same two woven containers, this time placed on small plinths. They contain an assortment of loquat branches, cut limes, cut blood oranges, cotinus foliage, blue delphiniums, yellow iris, cornflowers and 'Gold Medal' roses. The airy inflorescences of the cotinus combine well with the rusty brown of the baskets. Low, inconspicuous rust-coloured rectangular cake tins hold the flowers.

(Photograph courtesy James Manifold)

(*Left*) A tall tin pot makes a good container for a heavy piece of sculptured driftwood with a grouping of the highly perfumed 'Chartreuse de Parme' rose. Feathery kale on the left, and the mauve-pink rose 'Baronne E. de Rothschild', are mixed with a silver succulent on the right. Grapes cascading downwards tie in well with the container. Driftwood, grapes and silver succulents make excellent outdoor arrangements for barbecues and garden openings – but they need to be brought indoors before the birds eat the grapes.

(Photograph courtesy James Manifold)

(*Right*) A classic fibreglass urn contains groupings of dried wisteria vine, small palm spathes, pomegranates and quinces on skewers. I made this arrangement to add interest to a corner of the garden at the time of my eightieth birthday party and it lasted for eight weeks.

A large wire mesh basket with an attractive lid is filled with a medley of home-grown autumn fruits of various shapes and sizes – red table grapes, pomegranates, huge quinces, apples, green limes, oranges and grapefruit. Some of the citrus were cut open to show their interiors. Rose hips and autumn berries could also be used. Such arrangements, using a selected group of fruits, would last several months in the garden. I am fortunate to live in an area where there is an abundance of fruit and vegetables and where I can readily obtain unusual material that is too big or too small for sale.

A brass coal scuttle holds a collection of autumn flowers and fruits from the garden – orange lilies, tawny brown and yellow annual sunflowers, quinces on branches, purple grapes, myrtle berries, sprays of rose hips and kniphofias. Salmon-pink 'Interview' roses give way to yellow 'Mabella' and a couple of orange-red 'Mercedes' roses which tie in with the orange liliums.

Chapter 12

Winter Arrangements

In our mild Mediterranean climate we can always find something to use in a flower arrangement in winter. We have few frosts in Renmark but occasionally the temperature falls to –6 or –7° C. This can burn the winter-flowering salvias which, thankfully, usually reshoot in spring. I grow pots of white primulas, anemones and ranunculus, and can also rely on camellias, winter-flowering kniphofias and a succession of flowering blossom trees – starting in late June with *Prunus mume* and ending with the late cherries and crab-apples and double pink and red hawthorns in October – a period of four months. Euphorbias are handy and *Jasminum nudiflora* and early viburnums are good standbys. When winters are wet and not severe we can always find roses, for when pruning the roses I leave any bushes with buds and tackle them later.

Three terracotta pots hold fasciated ash tree wood that I've used in countless arrangements. Groupings of flowering aloe and leucospermum are joined by strelizias, three year old dried ornamental corn with oranges being the dominant feature at the lip of each container. An old pedestal gives height to the central arrangement and the loops give a feeling of motion between each section.

(Photograph courtesy James Manifold)

209

Lichen-covered taxodium branches in a modern earthy container holding stems of orange-yellow and green kniphofias at various levels to give impact. The pokers brighten the winter garden and are indispensible when flowers are in short supply.

Another petrol drum holds straight and twisted xanthorrhoea flower spikes with a base of lime-green euphorbia and ornamental kale. Only large country bush properties can indulge in this sort of arrangement.

Two simple, small round containers on a rustic bench hold branches of *Prunus mume*, the winter-flowering apricot that flowers in June and July and then becomes dormant, unlike almonds, plums, peaches and apples that come into growth immediately after flowering. A few early blue anemones, 'Winter Cheer' narcissus, mauve wallflower and 'Costa Rica' blue salvia stems help to brighten a cold winter's day.

Three lovely woven boat-shaped baskets on my old wooden red gum table house a winter arrangement. Parallel spikes of white japonica, deep pink peach blossom and pale pink almond blossom provide colour at the top. Flowers for the base consist of roses, camellias, nerines and salvias, which are set off well against a bamboo background. Some years roses continue to flower in Renmark until August, but in other years they can be frosted off in June.

several hours before arranging. They should then last for several days in a cool position. Their colour range is almost vulgar – but gorgeous.

Pomegranate is a very old plant famous as a symbol of fertility. The flowers last very well when picked. Long stems can be placed in water so that the lovely shiny foliage does not wilt. Individual fruits do not need water, however. They slowly dry and lose some colour but will last a number of years – useful when flowers are in short supply. Pomegranates were used both in flower and fruit by the Old Masters.

Poppies are a very old-fashioned flower, be they Iceland, opium, Shirley, Flanders or blue meconopsis. All need to have the stems held under a flame to seal the cut and are all best picked just before opening. Opium poppies, if recut, need to be burnt again before using. I think poppies are better in water than in oasis. Some of the huge double opium poppies with their curved stems and grey-green foliage are fascinating. Again, they were used brilliantly by the Old Masters.

Ranunculus keep well in water if picked when the flowers are half out. The new double camellia-like varieties come in a range of new colours and can last fourteen days.

Rhododendrons are flowers for cool climates. They last well if given deep water and a cool spot.

Roses are best picked early in the day, in bud form for loose-petalled varieties and one-third open for very double types. Put into water straight away and then leave in a cool, dark, draught-free place, or ideally a coolroom, overnight. I do not like picking roses after rain. It is best if they are left to dry out on the bush. If this is not possible, shake the buds with a downward movement of the hand to remove as much water as possible and dry them out under cover before arranging. If packing in boxes to take away, remember that roses packed wet, like fruit and lettuce, do not keep well. I de-thorn the lower stems after picking, but leave the thorns among the remaining leaves.

Salvias withstand drought well and are becoming increasingly popular. However, they vary in their keeping quality. Some varieties will not keep, others will last ten to fourteen days. Salvia expert Betsy Clebsch from California recommends re-cutting the stems under water. This does help quite a few varieties to keep very well. Many salvias are blue in colour, which is a great asset in flower arrangements, as blue flowers can be difficult to find. Spent blooms will drop, which can be a nuisance.

Scabious are a handy flower in pink, blue and mauve and last well if picked when opening.

Stocks are a spring feature. Unfortunately in the last few years there has been a great percentage of singles occurring and spoiling garden displays. Stocks can discolour the water in which they are arranged so it is best to change the water frequently. It is amazing how many early spring flowers, like stock, are strongly perfumed – **daphne, violet, boronia, sweet pea, jonquil, lily of the valley, wintersweet**, as well as **spring plum, pear, citrus** and **almond** blossom, to name but a few.

Succulents have become very popular for drought conditions. They can be cut from the parent plant and used in oasis where they will last for months, make roots and then can be planted out in the garden. The thick stems of some succulents can have a wooden skewer pushed into the base and then pushed a little way into the oasis. Many types last for weeks out of water. When taking cuttings it is best not to plant them for a week or so until the cut dries out. If soft, they can rot before rooting.

Sunflowers are again in vogue. The flowers last well in deep water but the foliage can wilt if it is soft and therefore must be removed. New buds will keep opening and the flowers with spent petals can have the petals removed, leaving an interesting seed head that will produce more plants next year. There is a beautiful strain of brown and mahogany coloured sunflower available which is perfect for autumn arranging.

Tulips are loved everywhere. The range of colours is enormous, as is the petal count. Tulips must have cool conditions and hate hot stuffy central heating. They prefer water to oasis and the leaves complement the beauty of the flower. They will droop quickly if they are put in a draughty position or exposed to the sunlight. It is best to use them showing the poise of the flower on the stem.

Yuccas need to be picked when half out and kept in a cool place. They are magnificent in church urns as they are so stately. They must be placed in a vertical position. Even one spike with bold foliage at the base can look great.

Zinnias are good for summer use, especially the cool soft green types. They last well in water or oasis.

Things That Don't Keep Well

Citrus foliage on long stems is inclined to curl inwards after a few days, and you are lucky if **duranta** with its blue flowers and orange berries keeps overnight. **Persimmon** foliage goes limp quickly, and the **soft spring growth on both evergreen and deciduous trees and shrubs** must harden off on the bush before it can be used successfully. This makes picking foliage in spring more difficult than at other times. **Wisteria** is one of the pleasures of spring, but the racemes must be fairly mature to keep. Putting the ends of the branches in boiling water helps. Even then, a couple of days will be the limit – just long enough for a wedding! A white Japanese variety has racemes over a metre long, a sight to see.

Staying with friends overseas, I remain surprised that when their gardens are filled with flowers they buy blooms from their florists and only use interesting foliage and grasses from their own gardens. I like to use only what I grow. I suppose it is the same as picking your own fruit and vegetables for a dinner party; it gives you a sense of satisfaction.

I have observed that guests entering a home almost always look at the flowers first. It brings the outside in and gives a lift to the setting. This can especially be seen in stately homes like Castle Howard where the huge urns of liliums, delphiniums and peonies in season are breathtaking and act as a foil to the antique treasures within.

Old houses with old furniture lend themselves to old roses and vases containing a variety of flowers and greenery. Modern, austere surroundings with a minimum of clutter can add drama by using bold colour schemes and contrasts in form and texture when making an arrangement.

Index

General Index